METHODS, SUBSTANCES, AND PROCESS OF PUBLIC POLICY

METHODS, SUBSTANCES, AND PROCESS OF PUBLIC POLICY

STUART NAGEL

Nova Science Publishers, Inc.
New York

Senior Editors: Susan Boriotti and Donna Dennis
Coordinating Editor: Tatiana Shohov
Office Manager: Annette Hellinger
Graphics: Wanda Serrano
Book Production: Matthew Kozlowski, Jonathan Rose and Jennifer Vogt
Circulation: Raymond Davis, Cathy DeGregory, Ave Maria Gonzalez and Jonathan Roque
Communications and Acquisitions: Serge P. Shohov

Library of Congress Cataloging-in-Publication Data
Available Upon Request

ISBN 1-59033-241-5.

227 Main Street, Suite 100
Huntington, New York 11743
Tele. 631-424-NOVA (6682) Fax 631-425-5933
E Mail: Novascience@earthlink.net
www.novapublishers.com

Printed in the United States of America

CONTENTS

PART ONE: METHODS

SECTION A: POLICY EVALUATION

Chapter 1

CONCEPTUAL THEORY AND POLICY EVALUATION[1]

I. DEFINING POLICY ANALYSIS

Public policy analysis can be defined as determining which of various alternative public or governmental policies will most achieve a given set of goals in light of the relations between the policies and the goals. That definition brings out the five key elements of policy evaluation:

1. Goals, including normative constraints and relative weights for the goals.
2. Policies, programs, projects, decisions, options, means, or other alternatives that are available for achieving the goals.
3. Relations between the policies and the goals, including relations that are established by intuition, authority, statistics, observation, deduction, guesses, or by other means.
4. Drawing a tentative conclusion as to which policy or combination of policies is best to adopt in light of the goals, policies, and relations.
5. Determining what it would take to bring a second-place or other-place alternative up to first place.

Other concepts that are often used to mean the same thing as public policy analysis include policy evaluation, policy studies, program evaluation, public management science, and policy science. One could make distinctions between those concepts as follows:

1. Policy evaluation emphasizes evaluating alternative public policies, as contrasted to describing them or explaining why they exist.
2. Policy studies includes describing policies, explaining their existence, and evaluating them.

[1] Modified from Nagel (ed.), *Policy Theory and Policy Evaluation: Concepts, Knowledge, Causes, and Norms* (Greenwood, 1990).

3. Program evaluation emphasizes evaluating a specific program like a halfway house in Chicago in 1984, as contrasted to developing general principles of how to evaluate.
4. Public management science emphasizes decision-making that is involved in implementing broader decisions, generally made by legislatures and agencies that have quasi-legislative authority.
5. Policy analysis emphasizes systematic analytic methods that can be quantitative or qualitative.
6. Policy science emphasizes quantitative methods.

Methods of public policy analysis refer to:

1. How to draw a conclusion as to which policy to adopt from information on goals, policies, and relations.
2. How to establish the relations between policies and goals.
3. How to determine what policies are available for adoption and what goals are appropriate to consider.

II. Defining Good Policy Analysis

The key characteristics of good policy analysis relate to validity, importance, usefulness, originality, and feasibility.

A. Validity

Validity in general refers to being accurate. In the context of policy evaluation research and its key elements, validity refers to:

1. The listed goals that include all the major goals and no non-goals of the relevant policy makers in this context.
2. The policies being considered should encompass the total set of feasible alternatives and no infeasible alternatives. Feasibility in this context refers to being capable of being adopted and implemented by the relevant policy makers and policy appliers.
3. The external consistency with empirical reality in describing the relations between the alternative policies and the goals.
4. The internal consistency of logically drawing a conclusion that follows from the goals, policies, and relations.

Validity can occur in degrees, or at least non-validity can. A valid study meets all four of the above requirements. An invalid study fails to meet at least one of the four requirements. A study is even more invalid if it fails to meet more than one of the requirements, or fails to meet a requirement by a large margin. Validity in policy evaluation is thus like equity where equity is defined as providing a minimum benefits level for all relevant persons, groups, or places. Thus, if that minimum level is met, equity is present although equality may not be present. There can, however, be degrees of inequity depending on the size of the individual deviations from that minimum level and the number of people involved, as is the case with non-validity.

B. Importance

On the matter of importance, that concept can be defined in two ways:

1. Does the research deal with issues in which there are big societal benefits and/or big societal costs being analyzed? Thus research on avoiding nuclear war is more important than research on whether a city should have a strong mayoral form of government or a city manager.
2. Does the research deal with a subject matter or a set of causal hypotheses that potentially have broad explanatory power? This is theoretical importance, as contrasted to policy importance.

There can be degrees of policy importance depending on the product of the total benefits times the total costs that are at stake. That benefits-times-costs criterion makes sense in judging the relative importance of two research projects, even though benefits-minus-costs is the criterion for judging which of two investments or alternative policies to adopt. In other words, if one research project deals with benefits of 100 units and costs of 150 units, and the second project deals with benefits of 10 units and costs of 8 units, then the first project is more important given the size of the benefits and the costs, even though the second project would be a better or more profitable investment. We would not want to add benefits to costs to judge importance since those variables are likely to be measured in different units that cannot be meaningfully added. In this context, however, different units can be meaningfully multiplied.

C. Usefulness

On the matter of usefulness, that concept should be considered a continuum concept rather than a yes/no concept. Usefulness or utilization at its lowest level involves doing a policy research project that is not in any way referred to by the people who make policy in the subject matter area. Nor is there any evidence that the policy makers were aware of the project, even though they did not explicitly cite it. That is clearly non-utilization. At the other extreme or the highest level of utilization, the research project converts the decision makers from being negative to being positive or vice versa on an issue. That is a rare occurrence and may never occur for controversial issues.

At the next to highest level is research that reinforces preconceived decisions. This is reasonably common. Some skeptics of the value of systematic policy analysis consider that occurrence not to be utilization. Policy researchers should, however, be quite pleased if their research accelerates a worthwhile decision that otherwise might not be made for a while. An example might be the research that showed more defendants could be released prior to trial without increasing the no-show rate, provided there is some systematic screening to determine who is to be released. Liberals found support in such studies since they wanted to see more defendants released in view of the presumption of innocence. Likewise, conservatives also found support in such studies since they wanted to see a reduction in the expensive jail burden on the taxpayers. That kind of reinforcement did accelerate the presumably desirable occurrence of increased pre-trial release with a constant or lower no-show rate.

At the next to the lowest level is research that is referred to by the policy makers orally or by being officially cited. The citing could be by either the majority group among the decision makers or the minority/dissenters. Either kind of citing is an example of low-level utilization, even if the research cited was not on the winning side, and was not influential enough to convert decisions or even reinforce preconceived decisions. This is also a common occurrence. People who are skeptical of the value of policy research tend to emphasize how common the lowest categories are of no citing or citing but no influence. One should, however, recognize that progress in dealing with policy problems may require many unutilized research projects before a research project is developed that does get well used. The policy research system is still a success if only one in ten projects gets used, if that one tends to produce benefits that outweigh the costs of the other nine.

D. Other Criteria of Good Policy Analysis

In defining good policy evaluation, one should add as a criterion the concept of originality to the concepts of validity, social/theoretical importance, and usefulness. Originality can be measured in degrees since all research differs to some extent from previous research unless an exact plagiarism is involved. Even highly original research builds on and synthesizes prior research. Feasibility is an additional criterion for judging proposed policy research, as contrasted to completed policy research. Feasibility is concerned with how easily the research can be implemented given the limited time, expertise, interests, funds, and other resources of the researcher.

In defining good policy evaluation, we should also indicate certain criteria that should probably be considered irrelevant. One such criterion is whether the recommendations of a research study have been adopted by policy makers, even though the policy makers show no awareness of the existence of the research. To be considered useful, the research must at least be referred to. A second irrelevant criterion is the direction of the research recommendations in terms of being liberal or conservative. That criterion is not relevant to good policy analysis in an objective scientific sense, since there is generally no objectivity as to whether a liberal or a conservative recommendation is better. One could argue that liberal recommendations tend to benefit directly more people given their mass orientation. On the other hand, one could argue that conservative recommendations benefit more people in light of the trickle-down theory, which says the masses are better off if well-to-do potential investors are encouraged to develop new technology and businesses. The other criteria of validity, importance, and usefulness do have some objective reality on which both liberals and conservatives can agree.[2]

---

[2] On conceptual theory in policy evaluation, see Phillip Gregg, ed., *Problems of Theory in Policy Analysis* (Lexington, MA: Lexington-Heath, 1976); William Dunn, ed., *Policy Analysis: Perspectives, Concepts, and Methods* (Greenwich, CT: JAI Press, 1986); and Yehezkel Dror, "Basic Concepts in Policy Studies" in Nagel, *Encyclopedia of Policy Studies*.

Chapter 2

THEORY OF KNOWING AND POLICY EVALUATION[1]

I. SOURCES OF POLICY ANALYSIS ELEMENTS

Where do goals, policies, and relations come from? The answer includes four main possibilities:

1. Authority: one or more persons, books, articles, or other reliable sources of information regarding the relevant goals, policies, or relations.
2. Statistical or observational analysis: the analyzing of specific instances in order to generalize what the goals, policies, or relations might be.
3. Deduction: the drawing of a conclusion from premises that have been established from authority, observation, and/or intuition.
4. Sensitivity analysis: the guessing of the goals, policies, or relations, and the determination of what effect, if any, the guessed values have on the final decision regarding which policy is best.

The four basic sources can be subclassified in various ways. For example, authority can be meaningfully discussed in terms of expert authority and general public opinion. Authority could also be contemporary or historical. Observation can be impressionistic or systematic, including statistical. Deductive approaches can be based on intuitively accepted or empirically validated premises. Sensitivity analysis is threshold analysis in which we want to know the break-even point, above which we should take one course of action, and below which we should take another.

What constitutes an authority on goals, policies, or relations? The answer depends on the subject matter. The Supreme Court is an authority, for example, on what goals are legitimate in satisfying the right-to-counsel clause of the Sixth Amendment to the Constitution. The Court has said that saving money is not an appropriate goal, but that saving innocent persons from being convicted is. If, however, the issue is not whether right-to-counsel should be

---

[1] On the theory of knowing in policy evaluation, see Dunn, *Public Policy Analysis* (Prentice-Hall, 1992); S. Nagel,*Evaluation Analysis with Microcomputers* (JAI Press, 1989); and Jack Rabin and Edward Jackowski, eds., *Handbook of Information Resources Management* (New York: Marcel Dekker, 1988).

provided but rather how it should be provided, then saving money is an appropriate goal. For this issue, the goals of a county board would be relevant because it generally appropriates money to pay court-appointed lawyers to represent the poor. Such goals might include satisfying the local bar while minimizing expenditures. The board might, therefore, decide on a salaried public defender system, rather than on a less expensive but less politically feasible assigned counsel system or a less legally feasible volunteer system. For other policy problems, the key authorities might be legislative opinion, public opinion, the head of an administrative agency, or the like.

Accounting is a variation on statistical analysis. Like statistical analysis, it involves aggregating data, but accounting data are generally more precise than statistical analysis that is based on averages or the fitting of curves to scattered data points. A public opinion survey is not a variation on statistical analysis in the context of the typology of sources. Rather, it is a form of consulting authority in which the authority is the general public or a special segment of it. A statistical analysis (as a distinct source of information on goals, policies, or relations) involves a cross-tabulation, an analysis of the variation between averages, or a regression-equation analysis. These forms of statistical analysis involve determining a relation that is relevant to weighting goals, deciding which policies are feasible to choose among, or relating a policy to a goal.

Deduction involves arriving at a conclusion from premises that have been established by way of authority, empirical validation, prior deduction, or intuition. The more acceptable the premises are, the more acceptable the conclusions should be, assuming the conclusions have been validly deduced from the premises. Deduction is especially helpful where there is no authority and no empirical data for determining the information desired.

In policy evaluation, sensitivity analysis is a useful source of information about goals, policies, and relations when authority, statistics, and deduction do not provide clear answers regarding them. Sensitivity or threshold analysis enables one to determine how much room for error there is in weighting the goals, listing out the policies, or measuring the relations. Often, the controversy over precision in these matters is wasted because, within the range in which the controversy occurs, the overall conclusion as to which policy or combination is best is still the same. Sensitivity analysis also enables the policy evaluator to convert difficult questions about goals, policies, and relations into relatively easy questions, such as "Is a given weight, policy, or relation above or below some threshold?," rather than, "What is the exact weight, policy, or relation?"

There is no need to argue over which source between authority, statistics, and deduction is the most desirable. Authority is clearly a big time-saver if an accessible and respected authority is involved. Deduction enables one to draw conclusions about goals, policies, and relations without having to gather original data but instead of synthesizing already known information. Statistical analysis does constitute a more ultimate, but more difficult, form of proof. In any concrete policy evaluation situation, the best source depends on the subject matter and what is to be done with it. If the policy evaluation involves constitutional policy, an appeal to Supreme Court authority may be most relevant. If it involves the effects of a strike in the coal industry on another segment of the economy, a deductive input-output model may be the preferable type of analysis. If it concerns the trade-off problem of inflation and unemployment, a time-series statistical analysis may be especially appropriate in relating inflation and unemployment to suicide rates, to the percentage of the two-party vote that goes to the incumbent party, or to other social indicators.

II. Overcoming Obstacles to Policy Analysis Knowledge

There are five key methodological problems in decision-making:

1. Multiple dimensions on multiple goals. This is the "apples and oranges" problem.
2. Multiple missing information.
3. Multiple alternatives that are too many for us to be able to determine the effects of each one.
4. Multiple and possibly conflicting constraints.
5. The need for simplicity in drawing and presenting conclusions in spite of all that multiplicity.

Decision-making problems often involve multiple goals measured on a variety of different dimensions, such as miles, hours, dollars, 1-5 attitude scales, yes-no dichotomies, and so on. Some of the ways in which multiple dimensions are handled are to (1) multiply the apples by two if you like each apple twice as much as each orange; then everything will be expressed in orange units; (2) ask whether the gain in apples from choosing one alternative is worth more or less than the gain in oranges from choosing a second alternative; or (3) convert the apple units into percentages by dividing the raw scores on the apples goal by the sum of the apples, and convert the orange units into percentages by dividing the raw scores on the oranges goal by the sum of the oranges.

We often do not know relation scores of each alternative on each goal, and we often do not know the relative weights of the goals. The key way in which missing information is handled is to allow the user to quickly and accurately determine the effects of inserting various values for the missing information. More specific techniques include:

(1) "What if' analysis, whereby the computer shows what would happen if we made changes in the goals, alternatives, and/or relations.

(2) Threshold analysis, whereby the computer shows for each relation score and goal weight the value that would cause a tie between the second-place alternative and the first-place alternative.

(3) Convergence analysis, whereby the computer shows for each goal weight at what magnitude the goal tends to dominate the other goals, such that nothing is to be gained by increasing the weight.

(4) Best-worst analysis, whereby the computer shows first what the conclusion would be using values that most favor a given alternative, and then the values that least favor a given alternative. The two conclusions are then averaged.

Decision-aiding software can help in allocating resources, as contrasted to the generally easier problem of just finding a best alternative or combination. A good way of allocating resources is to convert into percentages the raw merit scores of the objects to which the resources are to be allocated. One can then apply the percentages to the grand total available to be allocated. A good way to convert the raw scores into percentages is by dividing them by their total within the same goal in order to get part/whole percentages. Those percentages can then be summed across the goals, using a weighted sum in which the goals have different weights.

Decision-aiding software can help in dealing with constraints that require minimums or maximums on the alternatives or the goals or other conditions that must be met, regardless of how high the scores are on an alternative or on the goals. The constraints can be met *before* one allocates scarce resources or determines the relation scores. Doing so tends to result in giving an alternative more than it is entitled to when it deserves only the minimum. That result cannot occur if adjustments are made *after* allocating, so as to bring alternatives up to their minimums. The best ways of resolving conflicting constraints are either to expand the total benefits available or to reduce the total costs to be imposed so that all the constraints can be satisfied simultaneously. If that is not possible, then one can resolve conflicting constraints by developing compromises that satisfy each constraint in proportion to its importance. Other, less desirable, alternatives involve partially satisfying all constraints equally, or fully satisfying certain constraints in the order of their priority.

Decision-aiding software that is based on multi-criteria decision-making (MCDM) can greatly simplify the analysis of a variety of decision-aiding problems that have traditionally used more complicated and often less valid methods, such as arrow diagrams, payoff matrices, decision trees, optimum level curves, indifference curves, functional curves, and multi-objective programming. The essence of MCDM software is that it works with a table, matrix, or spreadsheet with alternatives on the rows, evaluative criteria on the columns, relation scores in the cells, and a summation column at the right showing the overall score or allocation percentage of each alternative.

Chapter 3

CAUSAL THEORY AND POLICY EVALUATION

I. ADOPTING VERSUS REJECTING PROPOSED POLICIES

A fundamental distinction in public policy analysis is the distinction between policy formation and policy implementation, or the distinction between policy causes and policy effects. That distinction is relevant to the concept of policy failure and the counterpart concept of policy success. Policies can thus be failures in the sense of never being adopted, or in the sense of being adopted but having unsatisfactory effects. The failure to get a policy adopted is a subject of particular relevance to political science, since adoption failure tends almost always to be due to a lack of interest-group support relative to the opposition for the policy being considered. Studying the interaction of interest groups is an important part of the mainstream of political science. That kind of awareness could be helpful in developing policies that are more likely to be adopted. Numerous examples could be given of highly praised policies that were adoption failures due to interest-group opposition that was not adequately won over, such as tariff removal in the 1930s, free-market farm pricing in the 1950s, and pollution taxes in the 1970s.

II. SUCCESS VERSUS FAILURE AMONG ADOPTED POLICIES

There are a variety of ways of classifying post-adoption policy failures. One dimension is in terms of the subjective intent of the decision makers versus the objective reality. In terms of intent, a policy is a success if it achieves its goals, and a failure if it does not. In terms of reality, a policy is a success if its benefits minus its costs are maximized, or at least positive, regardless of whether the benefits or costs were intended. A second dimension is in terms of quantity and quality. A policy is a quantitative failure if its achievement units fall below an intended or objective standard, even though there is some net achievement. A policy is a qualitative failure if it produces more undesirable than desirable results, as measured either by the intentions of the decision makers or by the objective effects regardless of intent. Since each of those dimensions involves two categories, one could have four types of policy failures by combining the two pairs of categories into a four-cell table.

A. Prohibition and Allocation Policies

A good set of categories, however, is one that suggests meaningful ways of reducing policy failure. The above categories may lack that characteristic. Showing too much concern for the intent of decision makers may, for example, lead one to suggest reducing policy failure by lowering one's goals, which is analogous to reducing crime by legalizing all activities that were formerly criminal. A more useful classification of post-adoption failure might be in terms of policies that prohibit or legitimize certain activities versus policies that involve allocating resources or effort. Prohibition or legitimation policies can relate to criminal activities, negligent behavior, breach of contract, economic regulation, transferring property, unconstitutional administrative practices, or other activities in which legal policies specify what is right and what is wrong. Post-adoption failure in that context refers to noncomplying behavior, which is behavior that does the wrong thing in spite of the prohibition or nonlegal recognition. Compliance is likely to be facilitated when (1) the legal policies are clearly specified and represent a minimum deviation from custom, (2) the policy makers are highly regarded and maintain a unity of support for the legal policies, (3) the policy appliers have time, financial resources, expertise, positive incentives, and negative sanctions in administering the policies, (4) the policy recipients have attitudes and backgrounds that favorably dispose them toward the policies, and (5) environmental conditions are conducive to compliance, including communications media, education facilities, and business conditions.

The opposite kinds of policies on the prohibition-allocation dimension are ones that involve decisions to generate various inputs in order to achieve various outputs. These policies include allocating resources to places or activities, deciding the degree of enforcement for given policies, or deciding how much due process to provide in order to protect the innocent from being treated as if they were guilty while apprehending and negatively sanctioning the guilty. At least in theory, such policies lend themselves to arriving at an optimum allocation of resources in which the nonlinear marginal rates of return are equalized across places or activities, or to arriving at an optimum level at which the marginal benefits equal the marginal costs. In practice, it is often quite difficult to use the methods of operations research or related fields to arrive at those optimum figures because of the difficulty of measuring the benefits and the costs, and of relating them to varying inputs. To the extent that one can at least roughly arrive at a notion of policy optimum, one can then measure failure for the these policies as the difference between the optimum and the actual. Thus, if the optimum allocation of a budget to a given anti-crime activity is $1,000 and the actual allocation is $800, then the anti-crime allocation is $200 off what it should be. If the $1,000 allocation would produce 50 crimes and the $800 allocation would produce 60 crimes, then the anti-crime allocation is suffering an opportunity cost of 10 crimes. Perhaps one should generally measure policy failure in terms of the degree of noncompliance, the deviation between actual and optimum, and in terms of opportunity costs, rather than on a dichotomy of failure versus success.

B. Deviation Between Optimum and Actual

The deviation between the optimum and the actual can generally be explained in two ways. The researcher may be wrongly attributing values or intended goals to the decision-makers, or the decision makers may be misperceiving the relations between their decisions and their goals. For example, if the optimum percentage of defendants to hold in jail prior to trial is 4 percent, and the actual percentage is 27, the deviation may be explained by noting that the optimum was arrived at by using societal costs such as the costs of incarceration and lost gross national product. The actual decision makers do not bear those holding costs, but they may be quite sensitive to the personal embarrassment of releasing a defendant who fails to appear in court or commits a crime while released. The problem under those common circumstances is how to internalize the external costs that the decision-makers generate. Doing so may involve trying to generate, some offsetting embarrassment by publicizing the holding costs that the high holders incur without a commensurate improvement over the low holders in getting defendants to appear.

The alternative or supplementary explanation is that the decision-makers do have the goals that the researchers attribute to them, but the decision-makers in this context do not have the facts regarding how their own behavior relates to their goals. More specifically, the legal policy makers may lack information on the high percentage of released defendants who appear in court without committing crimes while released, and they may lack information for predicting more accurately the probability that various defendants will appear. There are numerous policy situations in which policy makers could have their degrees of failure decreased or success increased by having additional social science information. When one talks in terms of the deviation between optimum and actual, one can readily see that social science and policy analysis can play a useful role in attempting to determine the optimum, and how the actual can be moved closer to the optimum.[1]

[1] On causal theory in policy evaluation and policy studies, see Thomas Dye and Virginia Gray, eds., *The Determinants of Public Policy* (Lexington, MA: Lexington-Heath, 1980); Judith May and Aaron Wildavsky, eds., *The Policy Cycle* (Beverly Hills, CA: Sage, 1978); and Helen Ingram and Dean Mann, eds., *Why Policies Succeed or Fail* (Beverly Hills, CA: Sage, 1980).

Chapter 4

NORMATIVE THEORY AND POLICY EVALUATION

I. PROFESSIONAL ETHICS

An interesting question concerns the ethical obligations of people who do policy analysis research. Such research often involves ethical dilemmas that relate to:

1. Whether one's purposes should include prescription or evaluation, as well as prediction or explanation.
2. Whether or not to work to maximize the interests of a political party, special interest group, or only general societal interests.
3. Focusing on intended consequences versus all consequences.
4. Efficiency versus equity as policy goals.
5. Evaluation versus evaluation plus diverse replication, as an obligation.
6. Cost-incurring versus cost-saving in research.
7. Whether or not to share one's raw data.
8. Research validity versus questionable findings that are not sufficiently questioned.
9. Whether or not to put people at risk in policy evaluation.

Openness may be the key factor underlying the resolution of ethical dilemmas in policy evaluation. The situation is like the blue sky laws that regulate the securities markets. A stockbroker can legitimately sell the blue sky so long as he informs potential customers and others what they are getting. Likewise, policy evaluators may be complying with basic ethical obligations when they make clear exactly what they are doing on matters such as in the above nine dilemmas.

Perhaps, however, to resolve these ethical dilemmas, more affirmative critique may be needed than just openness in reporting one's research. In the analogy to the blue sky laws, one might argue that a stockbroker should have an ethical obligation not to sell worthless stock, rather than merely an obligation to report that she or he is selling stock in a corporation whose liabilities exceed its assets and which has been taking a loss in recent years.

II. SOCIETAL VALUES

In discussing ethical policy analysis, one should discuss both individual and societal ethics. Individual ethics refer to standards of professional behavior, as previously mentioned. Societal ethics refer to the goals that society should be seeking and toward which public policy should be directed. On a high level of generality, one can say that society should be seeking to maximize societal benefits minus societal costs in making policy decisions. The concept of "societal" refers to the collective good in the sense of such ideas as:

1. The greatest happiness for the greatest number, as expounded by such utilitarians as Jeremy Bentham and John Stuart Mill and to a lesser extent by American pragmatists such as William James and John Dewey.
2. Bringing up the bottom with regard to those who are least well off, as expounded by John Rawls.
3. Doing things that make everyone better off or at least no one worse off, as expounded by Vilfredo Pareto.

Benefits refer to whatever the society and/or its leaders consider desirable. Costs refer to whatever is considered undesirable. Benefits and costs can refer to monetary or nonmonetary effects. Benefits and costs are interchangeable concepts depending on how they are worded. Thus, high employment is a benefit, and high unemployment is a cost, but they are the complements or inverses of each other. It makes more sense to subtract costs from benefits in talking about overall goals than dividing costs by benefits. The subtraction criterion gives more of a net gain to one's original assets when one project is better on B-C, but another is better on B/C. Other overall goals are also defective, such as (1) merely maximizing benefits without considering costs, (2) merely minimizing costs without considering missed benefits, (3) maximizing benefits subject to a maximum cost level, (4) minimizing costs subject to a minimum benefit level, or (5) maximizing change in benefits divided by change in costs. The fifth alternative is only a means to maximizing benefits minus costs. The third and fourth alternatives are sometimes justified because benefits and costs are often measured on different dimensions. There are, however, meaningful ways of considering non-monetary benefits and monetary costs simultaneously, rather than sequentially.

On a less high level of generality, one can say there are six sub-criteria beneath the overall criterion of maximizing societal benefits minus costs. The first three are sometimes referred to as the three Es because they start with the letter E and are associated with the field of economics. They consist of effectiveness, efficiency, and equity. Effectiveness refers to the benefits achieved from alternative public policies. Efficiency refers to keeping the costs down in achieving the benefits, generally as measured by benefits divided by costs. Equity refers to providing a minimum level of benefits or a maximum level of costs across persons, groups, or places.

The other three sub-criteria are sometimes referred to as the three Ps because they start with the letter P and are associated with the field of political science. They consist of public participation, predictability, and procedural due process. Public participation refers to decision-making by the target group, the general public, relevant interest groups, or other types of decision-makers whose involvement appeals to our desire to use democratic procedures for achieving given goals. Predictability refers to decision-making by way of following objective criteria in making decisions so that similar decisions would be arrived at by others following the same criteria. Procedural due process or procedural fairness means those who have been unfairly treated are entitled to have (1) notice of what they have done wrong, (2) the right to present evidence, (3) the right to confront their accusers, (4) a decision-maker who is not also an accuser, and have (5) an opportunity for at least one appeal.

On a still lower level of generality, societal values manifest themselves in specific policy problems such as how to deal with unemployment-inflation, environmental protection, poverty, crime, health care, freedom of communication, world peace, and reforming government structures. The goals of societal values at that level may refer to specific aspects of the three Es or the three Ps such as (1) increasing effectiveness by reducing unemployment and pollution, (2) increasing efficiency by reducing the tax costs of public aid and defense spending, (3) increasing the equitable distribution of crime prevention and health care, (4) increasing public participation in freedom of communication and the reforming of government structures, (5) increasing predictability and stability in crime prevention and the business cycle, and (6) increasing procedural due process in the administration of government programs and criminal prosecution.[1]

[1] On normative theory in policy evaluation, see Frank Fischer and John Forester, eds., *Confronting Values in Policy Analysis: The Politics of Criteria* (Beverly Hills, CA: Sage, 1987); Ronald Cohen, ed., *Justice: Views from the Social Sciences* (New York: Plenum Press, 1986); Paul Diesing, *Science and Ideology in the Policy Sciences* (Chicago: Aldine, 1982); and S. Nagel, *Public Policy: Goals, Means, and Methods* (New York: St. Martin's Press, 1984).

SECTION B: WIN-WIN ANALYSIS

Chapter 5

BASIC CONCEPTS ON WIN-WIN ANALYSIS

Win-win policy refers to public policy that is capable of achieving both conservative and liberal goals simultaneously. Examples could be given from any field of public policy, such as economic, social, environmental, legal, or political policy. Win-win policies should be distinguished from compromises, where both sides retreat partially from achieving their goals in order to obtain an agreement.

I. AN EXAMPLE IN THE FIELD OF ENVIRONMENTAL POLICY

As an example, the field of environmental policy involves both conservative and liberal approaches. Conservatives emphasize the role of consumers and the marketplace in restraining business from engaging in socially undesirable activities, like pollution. The liberals emphasize the role of the government in restraining pollution. Conservatives are especially interested in the goal of economic development, which may be interfered with by governmental restraints. Liberals are especially interested in the goal of a cleaner environment, which may not be achieved so effectively by relying on selective consumer buying.

A neutral compromise approach might involve giving business firms partial subsidies to adopt antipollution devices. Doing so would involve some requirements for receiving the subsidies, but less interference than regulation and fines. Doing so would help promote a cleaner environment, but there still might be evasions by business in view of the extra expense and trouble in complying.

A win-win policy alternative instead might emphasize subsidies to universities and research firms to develop new processes (that relate to manufacturing, transportation, energy, and agriculture) that are both less expensive and cleaner than the old processes. Those new processes then would be adopted by business firms because they are more profitable, not because the firms are being forced or subsidized to do so.

The new processes thus would achieve the conservative goals of profits and economic development, even better than retaining the present marketplace. Such a win-win policy also would promote the liberal goal of a cleaner environment, even better than a system of regulation, and without the expense of a continuing subsidy for adopting and renewing antipollution devices.

A specific example of such an environmental win-win policy has been finding a substitute for aerosol propellants and air-conditioning freon that is more profitable to manufacturers and simultaneously less harmful to the ozone layer, which protects against skin cancer. Another specific example is developing an electric car, which saves money on gasoline and maintenance, while at the same time not generating the exhaust pollution of internal-combustion cars. Developing hydrogen fusion or solar energy also may be examples of a less expensive and cleaner fuel for manufacturing processes.

II. Kinds of Feasibility

Win-win policies may be capable of achieving both conservative and liberal goals in theory, but not in practice. To be meaningful policies, they may have to satisfy various kinds of feasibility. For example, is the policy of developing solar energy for manufacturing feasible technologically? Is there sufficient funding available to subsidize the needed research if the private sector is not so willing, due to the risks, the large amount of money needed, or the long wait before payoffs occur?

Is there insurmountable political opposition from liberals who do not like government subsidies to make business more profitable? What about the opposition from conservatives who do not like government involvement in developing a research agenda? Is the program feasible administratively in terms of built-in incentives, or does it require a lot of obtrusive monitoring? Does the program violate some constitutional rights? Does the program make provision for workers and firms that might be displaced if the policy is adopted?

III. Creativity

Win-win policies may involve creativity, but developing them is becoming easier as a result of experience with the ideas. We now have many different approaches that can serve as a checklist in leading one to a win-win policy. For example, expanding the resources available can enable conservatives to have more money for defense, and liberals to have more money for domestic programs. The government sometimes can be a third-party benefactor in providing vouchers to enable both landlords and tenants, and also merchants and consumers, to come out ahead.

One also can deal with problems like abortion by getting at the causes. These causes consist of unwanted pregnancies that could be lessened through more effective abstinence programs and birth control. Thinking in terms of the goals to be achieved, rather than the alternatives to choose among, can stimulate win-win policies. So can thinking in terms of increasing benefits and decreasing costs.

Other approaches deal with early socialization of widely accepted values, technological fixes like the non-polluting hair spray, and the contracting out of government activities to private firms (which do well as a result of both the profit motive and quality specifications in the contract). Further approaches may involve combining (rather than compromising) alternatives, developing a package with something for each major viewpoint, having international economic communities, adopting a gradual or incremental win-win policy, and arranging for big benefits on one side with small costs on the other.

Win-win policy may be especially relevant as of 1994-1995 because the Democrats control the presidency and the Republicans control Congress. That division means that neither purely liberal nor purely conservative legislation is likely to pass in view of the Republican congressional majority, the availability of the filibuster to the Democrats in Congress, and the availability of the veto to the president. It is possible that some compromise legislation might pass, such as health care without an employer mandate or required forms of health insurance. Even better would be win-win policies such as promoting real economic growth through greater productivity related to increasing labor skills, new technologies, competition, and tariff reductions.

For further details on win-win policy, see Lawrence Susskind and Jeffrey Cruikshank, *Breaking the Impasse: Consensual Approaches to Resolving Public Disputes* (Basic Books, 1987) and such Nagel–Mills books as *Policy-Analysis Methods and SuperOptimum Solutions* (Nova Science, 1994), *The Policy Process and Super-Optimum Solutions* (Nova Science, 1994), *and Developing Nations and Super-Optimum Policy Analysis* (Nelson-Hall, 1993).

IV. Steps and Checklists

Win-win policy analysis in this context can be defined as handling policy problems by finding solutions that exceed the best initial expectations of conservatives, liberals, Republicans, Democrats, or whoever are the major groups, sides, or viewpoints in the policy dispute. Win-win is also called super-optimizing or doing better than the previous best of all major groups.

There are basically five steps to win-win policy analysis:

1. What are the major goals of conservatives, liberals, or other major groups who are disputing what policy should be adopted for a given policy problem?
2. What are the major alternatives of these groups for dealing with the policy problem?
3. What are the relations between each major alternative and each major goal? In their simplest form, these relations can be expressed in terms of a minus sign (relatively adverse relation) and plus sign (relative conducive relation), and a zero (neither adverse nor conducive relation).
4. What new alternative is there that might be capable of:

   a. achieving the conservative goals even better than the conservative alternative, and
   b. simultaneously capable of achieving the liberal goals even more than the liberal alternative? Whatever new alternative meets these two criteria is a win-win alternative or a super-optimum solution.

5. Is the proposed win-win alternative capable of jetting over various hurdles that frequently exist. These hurdles may be political, administrative. technological, legal, psychological, and economic in random order. Win-win solutions should also

consider how to upgrade workers and firms that may be displaced by downsizing due to increased productivity, free trade, defense conversion, immigration, merit treatment, labor utilization, creativity, and related factors.

To facilitate developing win-win alternatives, it helps to have a positive can-do attitude that it can be done. It also helps to have a checklist of types of win-win alternatives that have worked in the past. Such a facilitating checklist of types might include the following:

1. Expand the resources.
2. Find a third-party benefactor.
3. Set higher goals.
4. Decrease the causes of the problem.
5. Re-define the problem to emphasize goals rather than alternatives.
6. Increase the benefits and decrease the costs.
7. Socialize children in widely accepted values so the problems do not occur.
8. Find a new technology.
9. Contract-out via an auction to multiple firms with societal strings attached.
10. Promote international economic communities.
11. Arrange for big benefits on one side and small costs on the other.
12. Fully combine alternatives that are not mutually exclusive.
13. Develop a multi-faceted package
14. Adopt the win-win solution in steps, where the first step may be a traditional compromise.

For further details on the concepts, methods, and examples of win-win analysis, see:

1. William Baumol, Superfairness: Applications and Theory (MIT Press, 1986).
2. S. Nagel, Super-Optimum Solution and Win-Win Policy: Basic Concepts and Methods, (Greenwood, 1997).
3. Richard Noyes, Now the Synthesis: Capitalism, Socialism, and the New Social Contract (Centre for Incentive Taxation, 1991).
4. Lawrence Susskind and Jeffrey Cruikshank, Breaking the Impasse: Consensual Approaches to Resolving Public Disputes (Basic Books, 1987).
5. For a free copy of the handout materials used in the worldwide win-win and SOS workshops, drop a note to Nagel at PSO.

Win-win analysis can be applied to handling dissident faculty as an example:

1. A lose-lose situation is where a department or the university seeks to destroy a dissident faculty member. The university may suffer the stigma of being enjoined for violating free speech and due process. The faculty member loses money in obtaining an injunction and subsequent enforcement.
2. A win-lose situation. This is where one side thinks it can be a winner and the other side a loser. Trying to do so often results in lose-lose situation, as in litigation, strikes, and war.

3. A win-win situation. This is where the university can try to constructively encourage the potential creativity of dissident faculty. Doing so can possibly result in new ideas inventions, and institutions to the credit of both the university and the dissident faculty members. This is more likely to happen with administrators who have flexible democratic personalities, rather than authoritarian personalities. All administrators however, benefit from the funding, prestige, and quality students that go to universities that are in the forefront of new ideas, inventions, and institutional arrangements.
4. The same win-win thinking can be applied to dissident citizens in a country. The analysis is also applicable to other economic, technology, social, political, international, and legal policy problems.

V. Tabular Presentations

The above win-win matrix indicates that basic win-win analysis is about as simple as a tic-tac-toe table. A tic-tac-toe table has three columns made by two vertical lines. It also has three rows made by two horizontal lines. That is also true of a win-win table except it adds a fourth row for super-optimum solutions.

The first row indicates the types of goals to be achieved. The second column refers to conservative goals, and the third column refers to liberal goals. The first column indicates the types of policy alternatives under consideration for achieving the goals. The second row refers to conservative policies, and the third row refers to liberal policies.

A "+" sign indicates that the policy is relatively conducive to the goal in comparison with the other policies being considered. A "-" sign indicates that the policy is relatively adverse to the goal. Conservative policies usually do well on conservative goals, but not so well on liberal goals, as one would expect. Liberal policies do well on liberal goals, but not so well on conservative goals.

This is a classic tradeoff, where adopting either of the two policies means losing some of the goals. The result is usually a compromise, whereby both sides (or all major sides) lose something and gain something. Neither side is usually strong enough to impose its solutions.

Table 1. Generic Win-Win Matrix

Goals / Policies	Conservatives	Liberals
Conservatives	+	-
Liberals	-	+
Super-Optimum Solutions	++	++

Finding solutions where all major sides achieve better than their best expectations.

A win-win or super-optimum solution involves finding an alternative that is not purely conservative, purely liberal, or a compromise. It is, however, capable of achieving the conservative goals more than the conservative policies, and simultaneously capable of achieving the liberal goals more than the liberal policies.

The SOS thus receives a "++" on both the conservative and liberal goals. In that sense, it does better than the conservative best and better than the liberal best. It should also be feasible regarding economic, technology, social, psychological, political, administrative, and legal matters.

VI. An Example of the Generic Matrix

The table below applies the generic matrix to the problem of environmental protection, especially in developing nations. The main conservative goal is economic development, and the main liberal goal is a clean environment. Conservatives also endorse a clean environment but not as much as liberals. Likewise, liberals also endorse economic development, but not as much as conservatives.

Table 2. Economic Development Versus a Clean Environment

Criteria Alternatives	CONS Economic Development	LIB Clean Environment
CONS Marketplace	+	-
LIB Anti-Pollution Regulation	-	+
NEUTRAL Compromise Regulations	0	0
SOS Improved Manufacturing, Agricultural and Other Processes (More profitable and cleaner)	++	++

Notes:

The following points refer to Table 2 and other tables. They clarify the symbols.

1. Symbols in these tables include:
   C = Conservative
   L = Liberal
   N = Neutral
   S = Super-Optimum Solution
   #1 = Group 1.
   #2 = Group 2.
2. The + and - scores show relations between alternatives and goals. Those symbols have the following meanings:
   + = The alternative is relatively conducive to the goal.
   0 = Neither conducive nor adverse.
   - = Relatively adverse.
3. + = The best of the alternatives on the goal before the SOS alternative is considered.
   ++ = The best of the alternatives on the goal after the SOS alternative is considered.

The main conservative policy is to rely on the marketplace on the theory that consumers would not buy products that are causing unhealthful pollution. The main liberal policy is to rely on anti-pollution regulation on the theory that the fines, taxes, and other penalties will cause business to reduce pollution.

The usual result consists of compromise regulations that are not as severe as liberals would like, but better than nothing. The compromise regulations are not as desirable to business as no regulation, but better than what the liberals are advocating.

A win-win or SOS solution might involve public policy working through financial and other positive incentives to generate new processes for manufacturing, agriculture, transportation, and energy that are more profitable to business, but at the same time cleaner to the environment than previous processes. Such a profitable and clean policy would be an improvement on economic development and a clean environment.

An example might include the use of vehicles and machines that use less gasoline and oil, but are even more productive. such innovations are easier in terms of technology, funding, and other considerations for some kinds of pollution. Such innovations may also have a bigger impact on some kinds of pollution. The optimum allocation of incentive money is, however, a separate problem. The important consideration here is shifting conservatives and liberals toward such win-win solutions, rather than toward relatively ineffective marketplace and regulatory policies.

VII. SOS Applied to Economics

Economists (especially Keynesian economists) have argued that an expanding economy requires (or generally requires) deficit spending in order to stimulate the economy. If the government spends more than it taxes (an undesirable occurrence), then GNP goes up (a desirable occurrence).

Deficits are undesirable because they cause (1) government borrowing which raises interest rates which hurts the economy, (2) inflexibility in needed government spending because so much of the budget goes to pay interest on the debt, and (3) a class of relatively unproductive people who live off unnecessary interest paid by taxpayers. An increased real GNP is desirable because it means (1) more jobs, (2) higher wages, (3) more funds available for education and other worthwhile government programs, and (4) improved quality of life via private purchasing.

FEDERAL BUDGET DEFICIT AS A PERCENT OF GROSS DOMESTIC PRODUCT

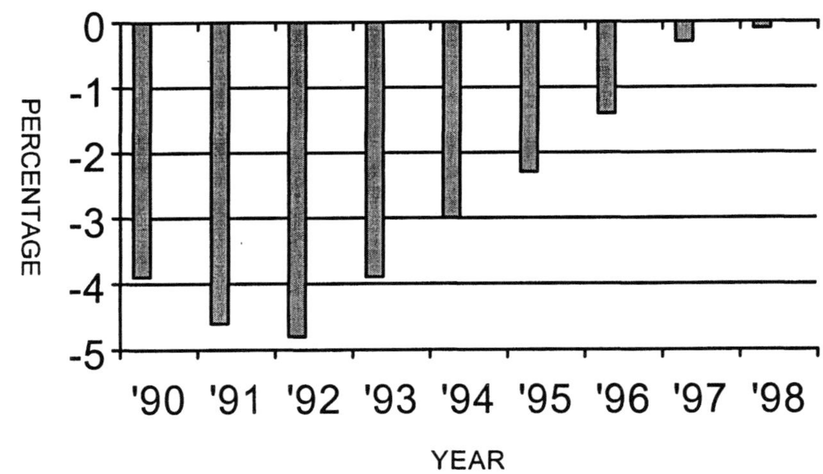

PERCENT CHANGE IN GROSS DOMESTIC PRODUCT

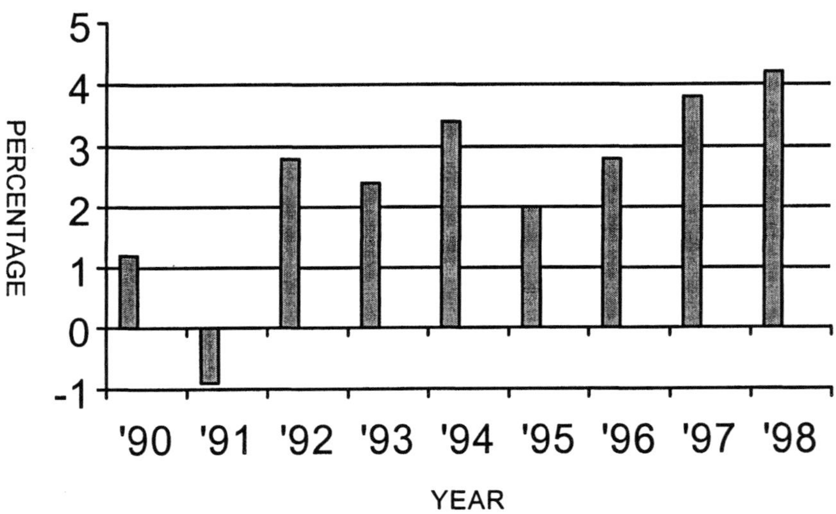

Traditional tradeoff thinking says we must accept undesirable costs to get desirable benefits. Win-win thinking says we can avoid the undesirable costs of big deficits and still have economic growth. The first graph above shows deficits turning into surpluses as of 1998. The second graph indirectly shows recent GNP growth from under $5 trillion in 1990 to over $7 trillion in 1998, at an increasing rate of growth.

This win-win occurrence comes about through improved technology, training, competition, free trade, and public policy. Those factors cause increased GNP. An increased GNP enables the government to have increased revenue from income taxes, and have decreased welfare costs. Those two factors lower the deficit, especially as a percent of the GNP.

Readers should not think that win-win analysis is biased against liberal economists like Keynes. For example, the Phillips Curve is associated with conservatives who say we have to suffer unemployment in order to avoid inflation. The autumn 1996 issue of Policy Evaluation shows unemployment decreasing in the 1990s to a generation low of 4.3%, and inflation simultaneously decreasing to under 1% which is almost nothing.

VIII. Compared to General Policy Analysis

Table 3. Basic Concepts in General Policy Analysis

I. Inputs

1. Goals	Y1	Y2
2. Alternatives	X1	X2
3. Relations e.g., 1-5 scale		

II. Processing

		Goals		III. Outputs: Totals (See Note 3)		
	Weights =	3	1	W=1	W=2	W=3
		Y1	Y2			
Alternatives	X1	4	2	6	10	14
	X2	3	5	8	11	14

Notes:

1. It may be highly questionable as to whether the policy analyst has used alternatives, goals, weights for the goals, and relations between alternatives and goals, on which large-scale agreement can be obtained.
2. The results are highly sensitive to the subjective alternatives, goals, weights, and relations.
3. The totals off to the right are calculated with Y2 having a weight of 1, and Y1 having a weight of 1, 2, or 3.
4. Processing steps for both tables 3 and 4 are

   (1) Decide on winning alternative: (a) Which one is best? (b) Which combination is best? (c) What is the best allocation?

   (2) Hurdles to Overcome: Economic, political, administrative, legal, psychological, technology, displaced workers and firms

   (3) What if analysis.

Table 4. Basic Concepts in Win-Win or SOS Analysis

I. Inputs

1. Goals	C, L, N
2. Alternatives	C, L, N
3. Relations	Just +, 0, or –

II. Processing

		Goals: C	Goals: L
Alternatives	C	+	-
	L	-	+
	N	0	0
III. Outputs	SOS	++	++

Notes:

1. The alternatives, goals, and weights for the goals are given by conservatives and liberals in congress, the courts, the newspapers, or elsewhere, rather than imposed by the policy analyst.
2. It is logically assumed that conservative alternatives have a relatively positive relation with conservative goals and a relatively negative relation with liberal goals, and vice versa for liberal alternatives. It is also logically assumed that conservatives give greater weight to conservative goals than to liberal goals, and vice versa for liberals.
3. With that reasonably objective information, one can deduce alternatives that are objectively win-win. If the win-win alternative dominates both sets of goals, then it makes no difference how the goals are weighted or totaled.

Chapter 6

WIN-WIN JUSTICE

I. DEFINING JUSTICE

Justice is one of the most important concepts in social, political, legal, and general philosophy, and yet it is one of the most subjective. It is easy to define justice with words that are like synonyms, but difficult to define justice in operational terms so one can objectively say that one public policy alternative is more just than another. Looking in a thesaurus or a *dictionary*, one would find justice defined in terms of fairness, equity, and other words that get at the idea of doing what is right, good, or better in social policy.

One could read whole books on the subject, not just dictionary definitions, and still not come away with any objective criteria as to what justice is unless one is willing to accept the assumptions of the authors of the books. Those assumptions are either on such a high level of generality that they are cliches or synonyms for the concept of justice; or they have built-in biases in a liberal or conservative direction. If so, they are acceptable only if one has a liberal or conservative value orientation to begin with.

Simple examples could be given of principles of social ethics that at first glance do sound like they have objective reality, but at second glance tend to have distinctly *liberal or conservative* biases. Liberal biases tend to favor the have-nots or the general population in a society. Conservative biases tend to favor those who are relatively well-off.

A good pair of examples are the widely accepted principles of Pareto optimality and utilitarian pragmatism. The basic principle of *Pareto optimality* is that social policy A is just if it results in at least one person in a society improving in terms of his or her well-being, and all other persons at least remaining constant but not worsening. Social policy A is better than B if two people rather than one person undergo improvements.

The basic related principle of *utilitarianism* is that social policy A is just if it results in improved happiness for a majority of the people in a society, while allowing the possibility of some people worsening but not below a minimum threshold. Social policy A is better than B if it promotes more happiness for more people.

The two principles conflict partly because one has a conservative bias and the other has a liberal bias. Strict Pareto optimality would consider progressive income taxes combined with government aid for the poor to be unjust because rich people might have a net loss between their costs and benefits. Poor people would have a total net gain that might more than offset the total net loss of the rich. There are more poor than rich, and a dollar given to a poor person may increase more happiness than a dollar taken from a rich person decreases happiness. Such a system of progressive taxes and government aid would be considered just by a utilitarian philosophy given its definition and its liberal biases.

The object of this article is to discuss a different way of conceptualizing justice so that social policies can be considered just or unjust, or can be considered more just or less just regardless of whether one has a liberal or conservative set of values. The object is not to arrive at compromises in accordance with Aristotle's golden mean or the moderation of Confucius. The object is to be able to simultaneously achieve or more than achieve the goals of conservatives and liberals, including doing well for both the rich and the poor at the same time.

II. The Objectivity of Justice

Justice refers to both procedural rules and substantive rules. Justice is objective if one accepts certain *assumptions:*

1. The conservative assumption is that the goal to convict the guilty is most important. This partly means to convict about 90 percent of all guilty defendants, guilty arrested, or guilty perpetrators.
2. The liberal assumption is that the goal to acquit the innocent is most important. This partly means to acquit about 90 percent of all innocent defendants or arrested persons.

It is good to *exceed both conservative and liberal best expectations* simultaneously. This relates >90 percent Convict Guilty. It also relates to >90 percent Acquit Innocent. Exceeding both expectations is good because it would be endorsed by the highest percentage. Assumption 1 is endorsed by 40 percent of the lawyer population. Assumption 2 is endorsed by 50 percent. "Do not know between 1 and 2," is endorsed by about 10 percent. Exceeding both assumptions is endorsed by about 100 percent, which equals 40 percent + 50 percent + 10 percent.

Just because *100 percent endorse* something does not make it objectively fair/good or objectively real/true. The correct phrase is fairer over the previous system, or fairer between two acts, or fairest of a set of acts. For some people, criteria are fair because they are *fairly adopted.* But if conservatives have a majority, liberals would consider it unfair. If liberals have a majority, then conservatives will consider what they adopted to be unfair. For some, there is no fairness in rules themselves (procedural or substantive), only in how they are adopted.

That which is just is that which *super-optimizes:*

1. A just policy is one that exceeds the best initial expectations simultaneously of conservatives, liberals, and other major viewpoints on the problem to which the policy relates.

2. An unjust policy is one that does worse than the worst initial expectations simultaneously of conservatives, liberals, and other major viewpoints on the problem to which the policy relates.
3. A policy that is not clearly just or unjust is one that neither does better than the prior best expectations of conservatives, liberals, and so on, or worse than the prior worst expectations of conservatives, liberals, and so on.

III. EXAMPLES

Three SOS or win-win examples can be given, drawing upon criminal, civil, and economic justice. The key dilemma or dispute in *criminal justice* is based on the desire of conservatives to have all guilty persons convicted versus the desire of liberals to have all innocent persons acquitted. The object is to develop procedures of super-optimum justice where there is improvement in the achievement of both goals over the status quo. One example is videotaping all trials to provide an easily accessible record of the testimony, thereby facilitating greater accuracy in both the convicting of the guilty and the acquitting of the innocent.

Table 1. Win-Win Criminal Justice

Goals **Alternatives**	**C** **Convict the Guilty**	**L** **Acquit the Innocent**
C Easier to Convict the Guilty	+	-
L Easier to Acquit the Innocent	-	+
N Between <C and >L	0	0
SOS OR WIN-WIN >C and >L	++	++

Notes:

1. Examples of rules that make it easier to convict the guilty include 6-person juries, majority votes, limited appeals, and restrictions on calling or cross-examining witnesses. Examples of rules that make it easier to acquit the innocent include 12-person juries, unanimous vote, easier appeals, and less restrictions on calling and cross-examining witnesses.
2. An SOS alternative in this context would be any rule that simultaneously increases the probability of convicting the truly guilty and probability of acquitting the truly innocent. Examples would be better training of jurors and judges on the meaning of various jury instructions or legal concepts and allowing the jurors to ask questions of the judges or lawyers to obtain clarification of legal concepts or evidence matters.

Table 2. Win-Win Civil or Tort Justice

Goals Alternatives	C Avoid Liability & Lawyers	L Compensate the Injured
C Difficult Liability	+	-
L Easy Liability	-	+
N In-Between	0	0
SOS OR WIN-WIN Reduce Accidents	++	++

Notes:

1. Having a defense of contributory negligence makes it relatively difficult for the plaintiff to establish liability. Having a system of no-fault makes it relatively easy for the plaintiff to establish liability. Comparative negligence is in- between.
2. Reducing auto accidents by improving cars especially refers to having airbags to protect drivers. Improving roads especially refers to having more median strips to prevent head-on collisions. Improving drivers refers especially to more severe penalties for drunk drivers.

The key dilemma in *civil justice* is based on the desire of conservatives to protect business firms and insurance companies from liability to consumers, workers, and others versus the desire of liberals to have injured consumers, workers, and others adequately compensated. The object is to develop procedures that will simultaneously save business from liability while saving would-be victims from injury. In the realm of automobile accidents, this may mean public policy directed toward safer cars, safer roads, and safer drivers.

The key dilemma in *economic justice* is based on the desire of conservatives to have individualistic private enterprise versus the desire of liberals to conduct business in a more collectivistic way. One form of super-optimum economic justice in this context is to have title or ultimate responsibility for factories, farms, public education, police protection, and other such societal activities in the hands of government while contracting out the operations for all such activities. Another form of super-optimum economic justice is to have a free market that is made competitive through well-placed government subsidies and tax breaks designed to stimulate multiple competing firms in every industry. Still another form of super-optimum economic justice in the realm of labor-management class-conflict is to provide for relatively high wages to satisfy labor, but relatively low payments to satisfy management. The difference is in the form of a wage-supplement voucher with strings attached designed to provide for the upgrading of skills through on-the-job training and the hiring of unemployed people, especially those outside the labor force.

IV. PRINCIPLES

These examples lead to three principles of super-optimum or win-win justice. All three principles can be illustrated by all three examples, rather than one example for each principle. The first principle is that an objectively just policy exists if the policy enables conservatives, liberals, and other major ideological viewpoints all to come out ahead of their best initial expectations simultaneously. The second principle is that an objectively unjust policy exists if the policy causes conservatives, liberals, and other major ideological viewpoints all to come out worse than their worst initial expectations simultaneously. The third principle is that a policy is neither objectively just or unjust if it enables one or more major ideological viewpoints to come out worse than its best expectations, although it comes out better than its worst expectations.

SOS or win-win analysis is difficult to refute for the following reasons:

1. If the solution really does *exceed the conservative* alternative on the totals column that uses conservative goals and weights, then it is difficult for conservatives to object to the SOS solution.
2. Likewise, if the SOS solution *exceeds the previous liberal* best on liberal goals and weights, then it is difficult for liberals to object to it.
3. There are not very many neutrals in highly controversial choice or allocation situations. Even so, SOS solutions tend also to *exceed the neutral* best even though that is not one of the definitional elements of an SOS solution.
4. It is difficult to criticize the weights that are used because those *weights are empirical* rather than normative weights. The weights are not saying that a given goal has high or low importance. Instead, they are saying that conservatives or liberals tend to evaluate the goal under consideration as having high or low importance. That is an empirical statement about what is, rather than a normative statement about what ought to be.
5. It is usually difficult to criticize the relation scores. They are basically rank orders or *relative direction* on which there is likely to be consensus, as contrasted to more precise measures over which there may be much disagreement, although not necessarily disagreement which makes any difference in terms of the bottom line conclusions. For example, no two people are likely to say that the Washington Monument is smaller than the White House. At the same time, no two people are likely to agree through observation as to how many inches high the White House or the Washington Monument is. In other words, the more precision that is demanded, the more unnecessary disagreement is likely to occur.
6. If there is disagreement over the weights or the relation scores, the disagreement can possibly be easily resolved through the *what-if analysis or threshold analysis*. It is likely to show that regardless which position is right, the bottom line stays basically the same as to what is the optimum choice or allocation, because that choice or allocation is influenced by so many other things.

Table 3. Win-Win Economic Justice

Goals / Alternatives	C Quality Goods	L Low Prices
C Marketplace Monopoly	+	-
L Government Ownership Monopoly	-	+
N Some of Both or Mixed Economy	0	0
SOS OR WIN-WIN Stimulate Competition (see Note 2)	++	++

Notes:

1. The marketplace may lead to monopoly or oligopoly by virtue of one or a few strong firms eventually dominating the industry and eliminating or greatly reducing quality and price competition. Government ownership normally means only one firm in an industry or in a region.
2. Competition can be stimulated by public policy through giving seed money to new firms. Also by requiring the sharing (at reasonable fees) of patents, railroad tracks, telephone lines, electric lines, and other facilities. Also from international trade in goods, services, labor, ideas, and factories.

Table 4. Win-Win General Justice

Goals / Alternatives	C Conservative	L Liberal
C Conservative	+	-
L Liberal	-	+
N Neutral	0	0
SOS OR WIN-WIN	++	++

Notes:

1. An objectively *just* policy has been found on the SOS row if the policy scores (1) higher on the liberal totals than the liberal alternative and simultaneously (2) higher on the conservative totals than the conservative alternative. In the above generalized context, that means scoring better than a 14 on both columns.
2. An objectively *unjust* policy has been found on the SOS row if the policy scores (1) lower on the liberal totals than the conservative alternative and simultaneously (2) lower on the conservative totals than the liberal alternative. In the above generalized context, that means scoring lower than a 10 on both columns.
3. A policy that is *neither objectively just nor objectively unjust* has been found on the SOS row if the policy scores (1) lower on the liberal totals than the liberal alternative, but higher than the conservative alternative, and/or (2) lower on the conservative totals than the conservative alternative, but higher than the liberal alternative. In the above generalized contexts, that means scoring between 10 and 14 on both columns.

Win-win solutions have not been achieved very often in the past. The lack of occurrence is probably not due to the lack of potential existence of such solutions. Rather it is more due to the disputants thinking in terms of either compromises or something like war, strike, or litigation. What is needed is more thinking in terms of the possibility of arriving at super-optimum justice. Normally one thinks of self-fulfilling prophecies as being something undesirable, as where the prediction of failure helps cause failure. A self-fulfilling prophecy can, however, be something highly desirable. For example, predicting the possibility of a super-optimum solution helps facilitate such solutions.

This article has sought to clarify the concept of super-optimum justice with examples and general principles. Traditional philosophy has been concerned with having a just society, economy, and polity. Perhaps it might be more fruitful to think also in terms of the super-optimum society, economy, and polity. Win-win ideas can perhaps help stimulate the development of more applications and details of win-win policies toward the development of a win-win or super-optimum society, economy, and polity.

For further details on win-win justice, see "Justice and Super-Optimizing Analysis" in Nagel, *Legal Scholarship, Microcomputers, and Super-Optimizing Decision-Making* (Greenwood-Quorum, 1993). For earlier background, see "Public Policy Goals" in Nagel, *Public Policy: Goals, Means, and Methods* (St. Martin's, 1984). For more recent applications, see "The Ten Commandments and Win-Win Analysis" in Nagel, *Super-Optimum Solutions and Win-Win Policy: Basic Concepts and Principles* (Greenwood-Quorum, 1997)

Chapter 7

Co-Effects Diagrams and Win-Win Analysis

In the Summer, 1999 issue of *Policy Evaluation*, there was an article on "Win-Win Game Theory." The article concluded that the MCDM matrix and the co-effects causal-path model were the best theoretical or methodological perspectives for analyzing policy problems to find win-win solutions.

The purpose of this short article is to apply co-effects analysis to key problems from the fields of economic, technology, social, political, international, and legal policy. The essence of co-effects analysis is to view conservative and liberal goals for a given policy problem as capable of becoming co-effects simultaneously favorably influenced by a win-win causal variable.

The six examples given here (along with references to previous articles) are:

1. The problem of inflation versus unemployment under economic policy.
2. Economic development versus a clean environment under technology policy.
3. Having a productive economy versus handouts for the poor under social policy.
4. Double voting versus non-voting under political policy.
5. Higher profits from free trade versus higher losses from free trade under international policy.
6. Repressing the sale and possession of illegal drugs versus the undesirable expense, corruption, and other side-effects of vigorous anti-drug enforcement.

Table 7 abstractly shows win-win generic policy. It shows that in the absence of a win-win causal variable, there is a negative non-causal correlation between the conservative goals and the liberal goals. That means one cannot be high on both sets of goals, but instead relatively high on one and relatively low on the other in a tradeoff manner. With a win-win causal variable, the answer is yes to the question of whether those two sets of goals can both go up simultaneously.

I. Prosperity Policy

Table 1. An Example of Win-Win Economic Policy

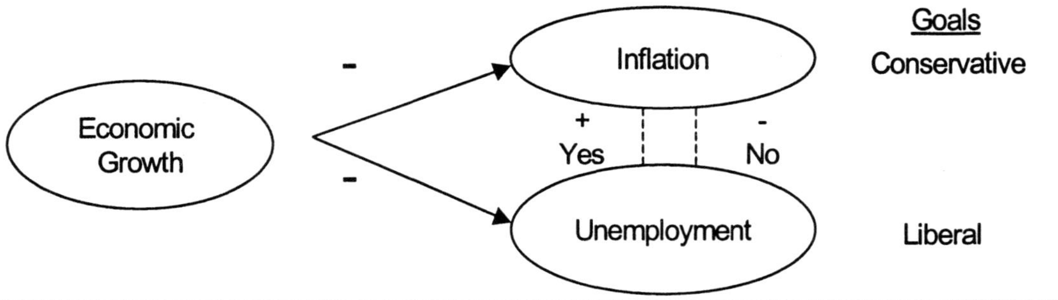

For further details, see "Win-Win Economics", 5 *Policy Evaluation* 5-21 (Summer, 1999).

Table 2. An Example of Win-Win Technology Policy

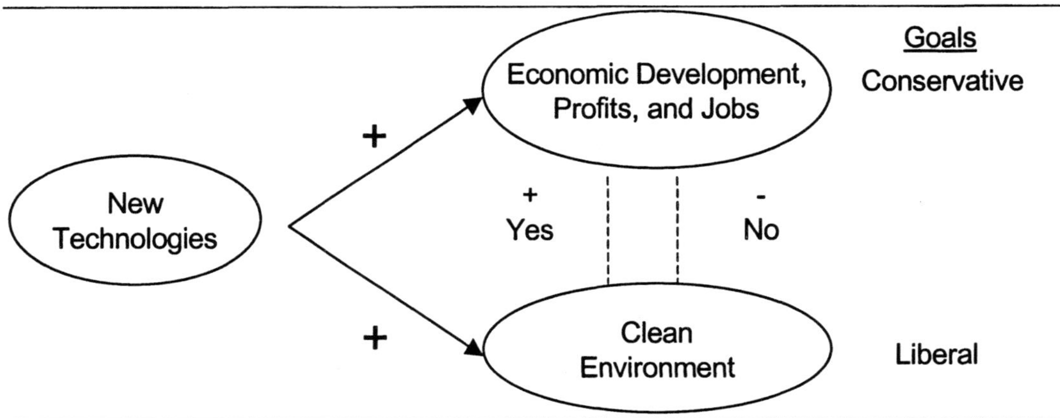

For further details, see "Win-Win Technology Policy", 5 *Developmental Policy Studies* 28-37 (Autumn, 1999).

II. DEMOCRACY POLICY

Table 3. An Example of Win-Win Social Policy

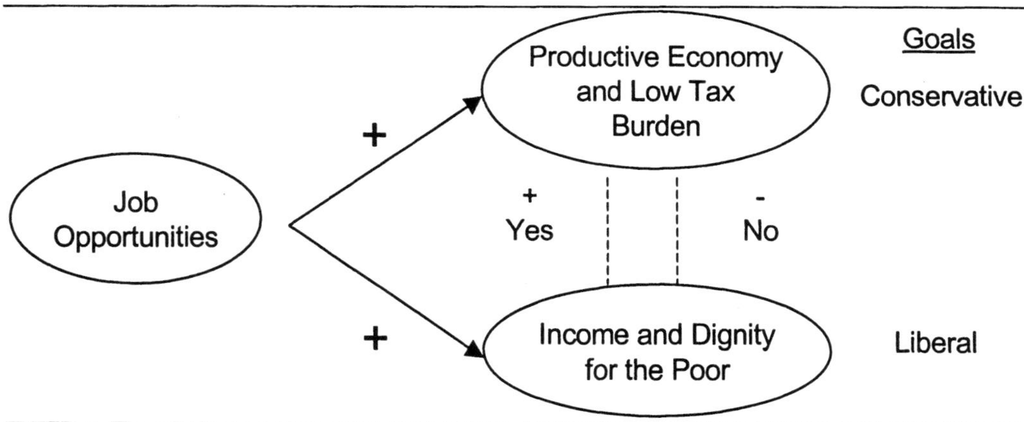

For further details, see "Social Policy: An Introduction" in Nagel (ed.), *Handbook of Global Social Policy* (Marcel Dekker, 1999).

Table 4. An Example of Win-Win Political Policy

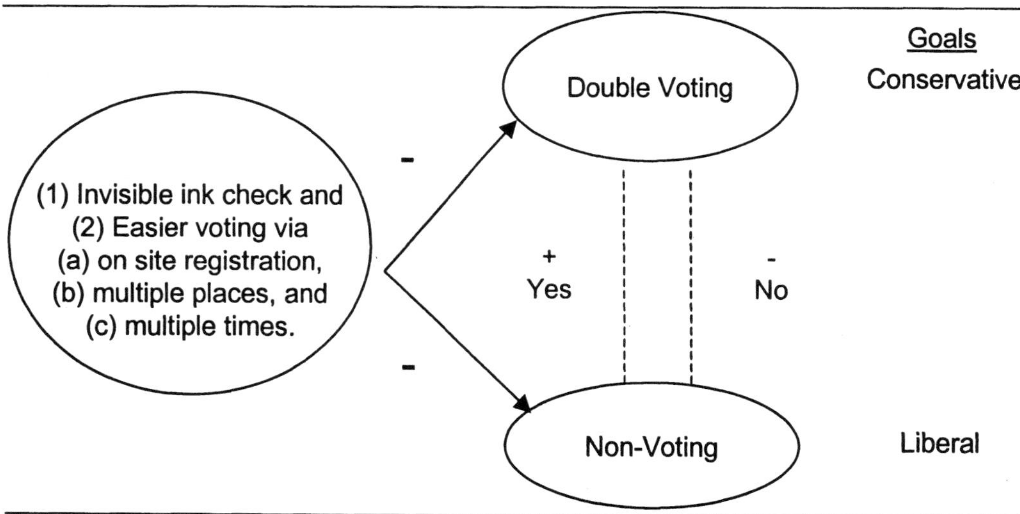

For further details, see "Governmental Reform and Win-Win Analysis", 3 *Policy Evaluation* 14-21 (Autumn, 1997).

III. Peace Policy

Table 5. An Example of Win-Win International Policy

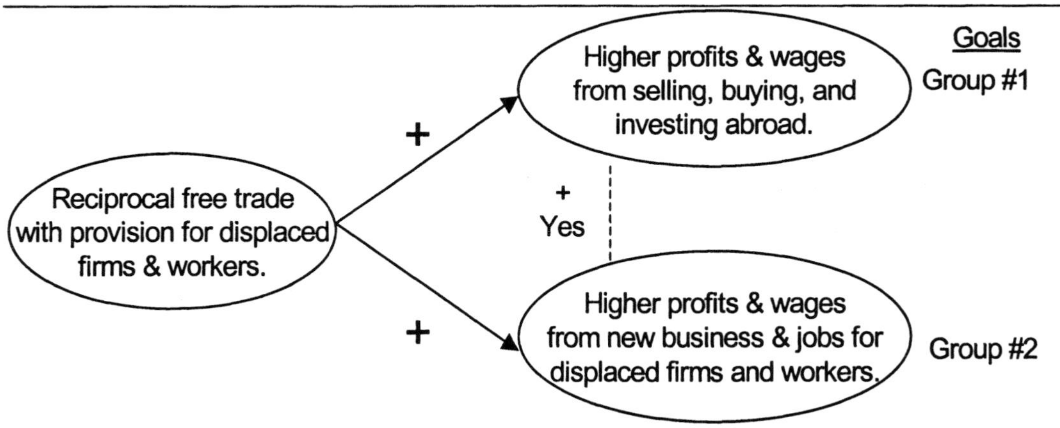

For further details, see "Mini-Symposium on International Prosperity and Exchange", 3 *Developmental Policy Studies* 9-24 (Spring, 1997).

Table 6. An Example of Win-Win Legal Policy

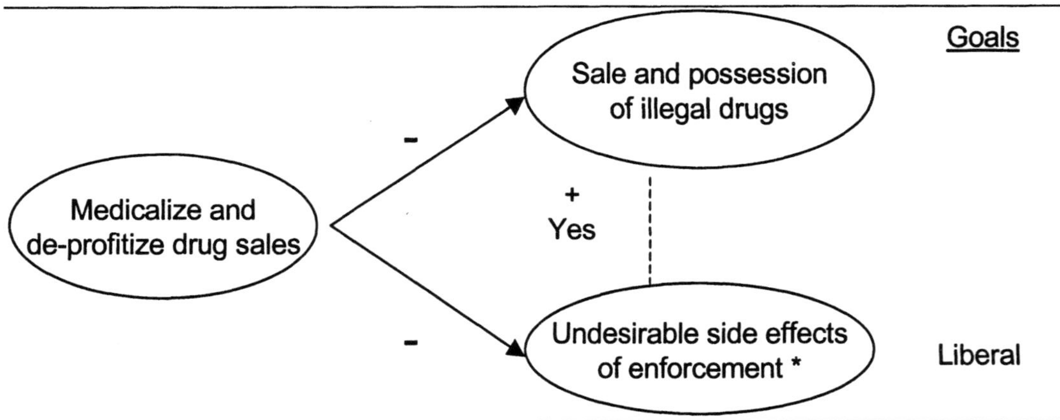

* Huge expenses for police, courts, and prisons. Also corruption of law enforcers, developing nations, and role models. Also AIDS, unemployment, crimes against property, and crimes against persons.

For further details, see "Legal Policy and Win-Win Thinking", 3 *Policy Evaluation* 12-25 (Spring, 1997).

IV. GENERIC POLICY

Table 7. Win-Win Generic Policy

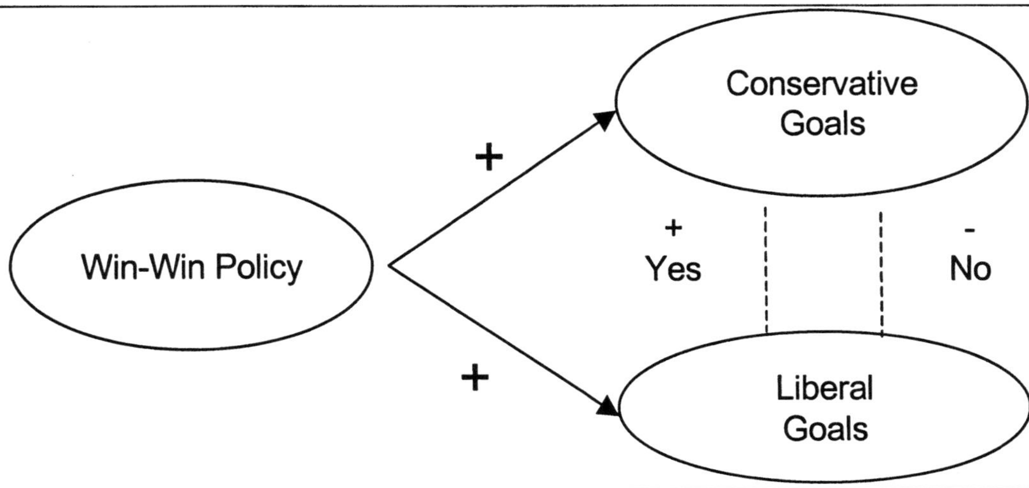

For further details, see "Generalized Policy Analysis", *Policy Evaluation* 33-41 (Autumn, 1996).

A Thought: To the optimist, the bottle is half full. To the pessimist, the bottle is half empty. To the win-win thinker, the bottle is half as big as it could be.

Chapter 8

SCIENTIFIC OBJECTIVITY AND WIN-WIN ANALYSIS

The purpose of this short article is to discuss the fact that there is a lot of subjectivity in traditional policy analysis that is largely eliminated by win-win analysis. This makes win-win analysis a win-win in itself generally by coming out ahead with regard to both results and procedures.

I. ANALYTIC COMPONENTS

In most policy analysis there is a great deal of subjectivity including the following:

1. It is highly subjective what *goals* the policy analyst will consider worth achieving.
2. It is highly subjective what *alternatives* the policy analyst will consider worth considering.
3. The winning alternative may depend on the relative importance of the goals. It is highly subjective what the relative importance or relative *weights* should be.
4. The *relations* between each alternative and each goal is also usually highly subjective, especially if measured on a 0-100 scale, 1-10 scale, or any scale involving magnitudes, rather than just relative direction. It is also highly subjective if the relation between an alternative and a goal is not close to true by definition.

On the other hand, in doing win-win analysis:

1. We do not decide the goals. They are decided by conservatives and liberals as determined by reading the New York Times, the Congressional Record, and elementary textbooks dealing with public policy issues.
2. We do not decide what alternatives should be considered. That is up to conservatives and liberals.
3. We do not weight the goals since weighting is irrelevant if one is trying for a solution that wins on all major goals.
4. We do not decide the relations. They are almost true by definition. They only use direction, not magnitudes. They are relative, not absolute.

II. Methodological Obstacles

In most policy analysis, there are many virtually unsurmountable methodological obstacles. They include:

1. Missing information, such as when recipients of questionnaire surveys totally or partially refuse to respond. Likewise, how alternative scores on various goals. [?] The results as to which policy to adopt may be very sensitive as to how that missing information is resolved.
2. Multi-dimensionality such as when different goals are measured in dollars, hours, ounces, deaths, robberies, education, health, etc. How those multi-dimensional goals are translated into a common unit can affect the results.
3. Even if the goals are all measured the same way there may be such a multiplicity of goals and alternatives as to cause great confusion with regard to overlap, duplication, gaps, and understandability.
4. After the result is arrived at, there may be little agreement as to whether it is really the best of the alternatives, even if there is agreement as to what the alternatives are and as to what the goals are.
5. There may be conflicting constraints that causes traditional methods to say that the problem is unsolvable, such as a minimum constraint of four units when there are only seven units to be allocated.

On the other hand, in doing win-win analysis:

1. There are no problems with missing information in such a simple analysis. There may be disagreement on whether a conservative alternative gets a score of 65 or 73 on a goal, but no disagreement that the conservative alternative has a relatively positive relation with the conservative goal, more so than the liberal alternative. The analysis is simple in that it does not involve any calculus, multiple-state leased squares, non-linear programming, etc., but it is not simplistic in the sense of leaving out important variables. In fact, important variables like due process and merit treatment are more likely to be included if the measurement system only requires relative direction rather than a factor analysis to four decimal places which tends to emphasize what is precisely measurable rather than important.
2. There are no problems of multi-dimensionality because all the relations are measured on the same scale of four symbols. The symbols are a plus sign for relatively conducive relations, a minus sign for a relatively adverse relations, a zero sign for neither conducive nor adverse relations, and a double plus sign for especially conducive relations.
3. There are no problems with multiplicity of goals or multiplicity of alternatives. We tend to group the goals in two groups, namely conservative and liberal. Likewise we tend to group the alternatives in two groups, namely conservatives and liberals.
4. There is some reasonable objectivity that the win-win solution is better than the conservative solution on conservative goals and better than the liberal solution on the liberal goals.

5. We do not have problems with conflicting constraints, although we could have in allocation situations such as a budget that is too small for both sides to come out ahead of their best expectations. We then seek to expand the budget, or to make the alternatives more effective and efficient at achieving the goals. That refers to the win-win alternative.

Chapter 9

FORESIGHT AND HINDSIGHT IN WIN-WIN ANALYSIS

Sometimes win-win solutions are criticized as being obvious. Other times they are criticized as being too subtle. They should be obvious at least as a matter of hindsight if they really are win-win solutions. They should, however, not be so subtle even as a matter of foresight. Indeed, the meaningfulness of win-win analysis depends partly on how simple and easy they are to develop as a matter of foresight and to understand as a matter of hindsight.

This article deals with (1) tests for win-win solutions, (2) making foresight easier than it is, (3) decision-aiding software, (4) post-development tests, (5) hindsight compared to foresight, (6) the increase in win-win thinking, and (7) how can win-win thinking be increased more?

I. TESTS FOR WIN-WIN SOLUTIONS

There are various tests of whether proposed solutions really are win-win solutions, including:

1. By definition, they must be capable of exceeding the best expectations of conservatives, liberals, and other major viewpoints simultaneously.
2. The solutions must be capable of being implemented. That means having economic, technological, social, political, international, and legal feasibility.
3. A win-win solution must exceed the conservative, liberal, or other alternatives by a large margin.

On the first test, best expectations are expressed in the goals that the disputants claim to be seeking, as indicated in legislative debates, books, articles, and press releases by ideological and partisan leaders. Goals can also include their real goals, which may sometimes differ from their claimed goals. Their real goals may have to be hypothesized for lack of objectivity. A win-win solution should more than satisfy both claimed goals and alleged real goals.

On the second test, economic feasibility includes lack of budget and displaced workers and firms. Technological includes engineering, natural science, and social science. Social includes ethnic, gender, and other group relations, and also socialization and family relations.

Political includes government structures, electoral processes, and public administration. International includes all the feasibility institutions but on an international level. Legal includes constitutional, statutory, and judge-made law. For further details, see Nagel, Public Policy Feasibility: Hurdles to Overcome (Nova Science, 2000).

On the third test, "large" margin in this context means being insensitive to reasonable changes in (1) scoring relations between alternatives and goals, (2) weighting the goals, or (3) changing the alternatives or goals. This insensitivity regarding small changes or unreasonable changes is virtually the equivalent of saying the win-win solution is obvious, at least as a matter of hindsight.

II. Making Foresight Easier Than It Is

As a hindsight matter, win-win solutions are thus by definition required to be obvious. As a foresight matter, they should also be close to obvious or capable of being easily generated. That is where checklists and typologies can be useful. Such checklists indicate types of win-win solutions that have been developed in the past. This includes a typology like the following:

I. More Resources to Satisfy All Sides

1. Expanding the Resources.
2. Third-Party Benefactor.
3. Well-Placed Incentives.
4. Win-win Allocation by Expanding the Budget.

II. More Effectiveness In Achieving Goals.

5. Setting Higher Goals.
6. Decreasing the Causes of Conflict.
7. Redefining the Problem in Terms of Goals.
8. Early Socialization.
9. The Technological Fix.

III. More Efficiency.

10. Increasing Benefits and Decreasing Costs.
11. Contracting Out.
12. International Economic Communities.
13. Win-Win Allocation by Increasing the Relation Scores.
14. Performance Payment.

IV. More Combinations of Alternatives of Alternatives.

15. Big Benefits on One Side, Small Costs on the Other.
16. Combining Alternatives.
17. Developing a Multi-faceted Package.
18. Sequential Win-Win.

For further details, see Nagel, Creativity and Public Policy: Generating Super-Optimum Solutions (Ashgate, 2000).

Other procedures for making win-win foresight easier than it is besides this kind of checklist are:

1. Working with a win-win matrix that shows goals on the columns, alternatives on the rows, and relations between alternatives and goals in the cells.
2. Working with conservative goals as a set rather than individually and likewise with liberal goals. One can also work with conservative alternatives as a set, and likewise with liberal alternatives. The goals and alternatives can be considered separately if doing so will affect the bottom line on what is a win-win solution.
3. Working with pluses and minuses to show direction of the relations, rather than with numbers to show the magnitude of the relations unless magnitudes would affect the bottom line.
4. Finding a win-win solution that dominates the alternatives on the conservative set of goals and that dominates the alternatives on the liberal set of goals, rather than other more complicated solutions.
5. Reading prior methods literature on win-win analysis such as Lawrence Susskind et al. (eds.), The Consensus Building Handbook: A Comprehensive Guide to Reaching Agreement (Sage, 1999), Nagel, Super-Optimum Solutions and Win-Win Policy: Basic Concepts and Principles (Quorum-Greenwood, 1997).
6. Reading prior substance literature and having relevant experiences in the subject matter area in which one is seeking a super-optimum solution. That could also include some awareness of other subject matter areas so that one can reason by analogy. For a variety of subject matter applications see Nagel, Peace, Prosperity, and Democracy: Win-Win Analysis (Lexington Books, 2000).
7. Making use of decision-aiding software, as described below.

III. Decision-Aiding Software

On the third test of sensitivity analysis, that is where super-optimizing software can be especially helpful. Such software can quantify how much better the second-place alternative has to do to become tied with the first-place alternative, or how much worse the first-place alternative has to do in order to become tied with the second-place alternative. The software does so by quantifying the weights of the goals and the relations between alternatives and goals.

The goals are weighted in accordance with the following principles:

1. Weights of goals are scored on a 3, 2, 1 scale where 3 is highly important to the one doing the weighting, 2 is middling important, and 1 is relatively not so important, but still having positive value.
2. Conservatives give conservative goals a weight of 3, and they give liberal goals a weight of 1. Liberals give liberal goals a weight of 3, and they give conservative goals a weight of 1. Neutrals give conservative and liberal goals the same weight which is generally a middling weight of 2.

3. Those are the default weights. If there is empirical evidence to indicate that conservatives and liberals are further apart or closer together, then adjust the weights appropriately, although retaining a maximum of 3 and a minimum of 0.

The relations between alternatives and goals are weighted in accordance with the following principles:

1. Relations are either positive or negative. Positive means the alternative is conducive to achieving the goal. Negative means the alternative is adverse to achieving the goal.
2. Positive relations can be either highly positive (scored ++ or 5), or mildly positive (scored + or 4). Negative relations are either highly negative (scored – or 1), or mildly negative (scored – or 2). Relations can also be neither conducive nor adverse (scored 0 or 3).
3. These are default scores. They can be adjusted upward or downward in light of empirical evidence while preserving internal consistency and a scale in which 5 is the maximum and 0 is the minimum.

The super-optimizing software supplements that kind of quantification of weights and relations by adding weighted relation-scores across each alternative. Doing so arrives at conservative and liberal total scores for each alternative and for the proposed win-win alternative. The software can then algebraically determine how the weights or relations need to change upward or downward to generate a tie between any alternative and the win-win alternative. If a tie can be easily generated without violating internal consistency or obvious empirical reality, then the proposed win-win alternative is too sensitive or shaky to be considered a win-win alternative.

The super-optimizing software can also perform other functions which may sometimes or frequently be useful such as:

1. There may be more than two basic sets of goals or alternatives. Human reasoning may then need to be supplemented by the computer's greater ability to deal with multiplicity.
2. The scoring systems on the goals may not all be 1-5 scoring systems. They may involve time, money, height, heaviness, or other multi-dimensions. The software provides for a part/whole percentaging system that can make multi-dimensionality commensurate.
3. If there are only two sets of goals and alternatives and 1-5 scales, there may be no missing information. In more complicated situations, there may be cells with question marks in the win-win matrix. The software can deal with missing information both algebraically and graphically, including multiple missing information.
4. Problems that involve allocating money, people, or other scarce resources to various categories are more complicated than problems that only involve deciding which of a few alternatives should be adopted. Allocation problems can theoretically involve an infinite number of alternatives. The software can deal with win-win allocation situations by developing new ways to increase the budget, or by developing new

ways to increase the effectiveness of the alternatives on the goals without increasing the budget. Doing so can enable all major sides to achieve their allocation goals beyond their best expectations.

5. Some problems involve complicated constraints such as maximums that must not be exceeded or minimums that must not be under-reached on either the goals or the alternatives. The software also deals with such constraints, including conflicting constraints. For more details on the super-optimizing software, see Nagel and Matthew Beth, Super-Optimizing Software, (Nova Science 2000) and Nagel, Policy Analysis Methods and Super-Optimum Solutions (Nova Science 1994).

IV. Post-Development Tests

We could have a second analogous set of three tests for a win-win solution subsequent to passing the above three tests. The above first set of three tests would be pre-development tests of the win-win solution. The second set would be post-development. The second set would involve the following:

1. After being developed, a win-win solution should actually bring win-win benefits in the sense of actually (not just theoretically) exceeding the best expectations of conservatives, liberals, and other major viewpoints.
2. In order to have those win-win effects, the win-win proposal has to be adopted. It is not enough that it just be theoretically feasible in the sense of economic, technology, social, political, international, and legal feasibility. It must also be actually adopted by the legislature on other decision-makers.
3. It is also not enough to satisfy a theoretical sensitivity test performed by a computer simulation. The win-win proposal must also be adopted and have win-win effects for some minimum period of time before it is considered obsolete either because it subsequently fails due to unforeseen complications or because it does well but some newer proposal does even better. Perhaps a win-win solution should meet a test of adoption with win-win effects for at least six months before it gets thrown out or upstaged. If it does perform well for six months, then it can at least qualify as an historical or past win-win solution. It does not have to be performing in a super-optimizing way forever. Eternal win-win performance would be contrary to the fact that we know win-win solutions are frequently improved upon before they are developed or adopted. They are even more frequently improved upon by post-adoption experience.

V. Hindsight is Easier, But Not Necessarily So Much

The story of Columbus and the egg is a good example of how much easier hindsight is than foresight, and how solutions usually or frequently look obvious as a matter of hindsight. When Columbus returned to Spain from the Western Hemisphere, there were a lot of people around the court who were jealous of the admiration he was receiving from King Ferdinand

and Queen Isabella. At a dinner honoring Columbus, one of his detractors said bumping into that land mass did not deserve credit since it was virtually impossible to miss it if one simply sailed west from Spain. This is quite true since the only way one could somehow miss the Western Hemisphere land mass was by going around Cape Horn south of Argentina or going through the Arctic straits north of Canada in the summertime, but probably only with the aid of an ice breaker.

Columbus's response was to say you are quite right as a matter of hindsight now that you have a better idea that there is this land mass out there, but we did not know about this as a matter of foresight. To illustrate his point, Columbus challenged his detractor to make an egg stand on its edge. His detractor tried repeatedly, but the egg kept falling over. Columbus then tapped the edge of the egg to knock out a small piece. The egg was then easily able to stand upright. The frustrated detractor said, "Oh that is so obvious."

This example is less relevant to win-win analysis than it appears to be at first glance. Win-win solutions are indeed usually obvious as a matter of hindsight. It is, however, undesirable if they are not so obvious also as a matter of foresight. Good win-win analysis should not be so subtle or technical that it can only be done by rocket scientists or the policy-analysis equivalent. Win-win analysis should be simple enough to be done by virtually anybody with a minimum level of common sense. That means possessing a degree of knowledge and intelligence that is widespread or common. Win-win analysis is not supposed to be a game designed to embarrass detractors. It should be an approach that will enable better policy to be arrived at as quickly as possible for dealing with problems of violence, poverty, disease, illiteracy, dictatorship, and other social problems.

VI. Win-Win is Increasing and Why

One might then logically ask how can average people get into win-win analysis? The answer is partly that they are already doing so, as indicated by over two dozen mentions of win-win analysis in recent issues of Policy Evaluation and Creativity Plus. Some of those mentions may not completely satisfy the above tests. They are, however, moves in the right direction. That movement toward more win-win thinking over the past five or so years is partly due to:

1. The development of dispute resolution theory and principles.
2. The development of theory and principles of growth economics.
3. Decision-aiding software.
4. The end of the adversarial cold war.
5. Free trade and its mutual benefits.

Liberals and conservatives are also coming together on the desirability of various public policies on which they were formerly sharply divided, such as:

1. Competition as in airline and trucking deregulation. Also deregulation of electricity selling, telephoning, and cable TV. This covers the important industries of transportation, power, and communication. Business and consumers are both looking

for lower prices and better products through competition among suppliers. Some businesses would also like freer entry into these industries. Even the existing firms may be better off by renting out their infrastructures.

2. Doing things for the poor such as employment facilitators for people on public aid. This includes outreach programs to enable the poor to fully qualify for university admission and for employment tests.
3. Vouchers that involve government money but are spent in the private sector for housing, food, minimum wages, training, and secular education.
4. Prohibiting discrimination against women and minorities for political reasons and economic reasons, as well as moral-ethical reasons. Business would like to hire on merit and sell where the money is without fear of being boycotted by dominant white males.

VII. How Increase It More?

These are economic, technological, social, political, and international forces that are helping to move policy analysis and layman thinking in a win-win direction. What can be done by people in the policy studies field to accelerate this movement? First, we should note that the movement toward win-win thinking is worth accelerating almost by definition. How can anyone object to conservatives, liberals, and other major viewpoints really all coming out ahead of their best initial expectations simultaneously? We are talking about mainstream viewpoints. We are not talking about extremists coming out ahead of their best expectations. Almost by definition, an extremist is partly one who so hates conservatives, liberals, or other major viewpoints that the extremist would be willing to suffer substantial personal losses or opportunity costs to keep those viewpoints from coming out ahead of their best expectations.

As for what people in the policy studies can do to accelerate win-win thinking, the following might be helpful:

1. Writing articles, book chapters, journals, and books that deal with win-win thinking. That includes edited books with a variety of applications to different policy fields or regions of the world.
2. Conducting workshops, classes, courses, distance learning, and other forms of teaching which include win-win analysis as part of the teaching. Training the trainers may be especially important. That is one of the activities of the PSO workshop program.
3. Points 1 and 2 deal with research and teaching. A third point in the academic world would logically be service activities. That means doing relevant consulting work for government agencies. It could also mean participating in think-tank activities for political parties and interest groups. It could mean inserting win-win thinking into advising businesses, not-for-profit corporations, and others when it comes to negotiation, mediation, and other forms of dispute resolution.
4. A fourth activity that may be quite relevant is research, teaching, and service that relates to the subject of creativity. That subject may be especially important to

developing win-win solutions. We mentioned above, however, that checklists are constantly being improved upon to make it easier to draw upon past creativity.

5. The above ideas tend to emphasize win-win substance. We also need research and teaching on the psychology, methodology, philosophy, and other aspects of win-win thinking that cut across policy fields, subject matters, regions, and scholarly disciplines.

We might be able to reduce to one word or a phrase what is most relevant to converting win-win hindsight to win-win foresight, which means the same thing as facilitating win-win thinking. The one word or phrase might be "positive-thinking" about win-win analysis. That means thinking that a win-win solution might be possible when faced with a policy problem. The more one thinks it is possible, the greater the probability is for finding such a solution. This is an area where the idea of a self-fulfilling prophecy seems to be especially applicable. If one predicts that a win-win solution cannot be done for whatever reason, then it probably will not be done, at least not by the predictor. If on the other hand, one predicts that it can be done, then a win-win prediction is likely to lead to a win-win solution.

VIII. Win-Win Mentions As A Form of Policy Evaluation

This is a continuation of the 27 win-win mentions on page 4 of the Summer 2000 issue of Creativity Plus and three back issues of Policy Evaluation, including Summer 2000 (page 39), Spring 2000 (page 36), and Winter 1999 (page 31).

28. "A win-win situation for Buchanan. He will gain access to dozens of new state party mailing lists, contributors lists, e-mail lists, and eager volunteers. That means that no matter what else happens, Buchanan wins." The Nation, November 22, 1999. That does not make it a win-win situation if the situation works to the detriment of the general public as well as the George W. Bush candidacy. Win-win situations require all major players to come out ahead of their best initial expectations simultaneously.

29. "Pollution reduction spurs the economy by creating jobs in clean energy industries, improving public health, and reducing reliance on foreign oil." TomPaine.com of the Florence Fund in the New York Times, May 2000. To be a win-win, pollution reduction should also be profitable for the business firms that reduce their pollution. This may require government money to fund research on new processes that are simultaneously cleaner and more profitable.

30. "The win-win approach is the promising way to go. The argument that constraints preclude such opportunities implies that all options for getting closer to the frontier (or moving that frontier) have been exhausted. That is an example of what has been called anticipatory surrender."

William Baumol, award-winning Princeton economist and former AEA president.

PART TWO: SUBSTANCE

SECTION A: DEVELOPMENTAL POLICY

Chapter 10

WIN-WIN ECONOMIC GROWTH POLICY

I. WHAT IS ECONOMIC GROWTH?

Economic growth can be defined as increase in the gross national income adjusted for inflation. National income is used in this sense as a generic concept covering income earned by people from the nation regardless where they earn it, or income earned within the nation by people who may or may not be citizens.

Economic growth can also be defined in terms of increase in gross national income divided by the total population. That is income per capita. It takes into consideration that economic growth is not very meaningful if it is exceeded by an increase in the inflation rate or the population growth rate.

Economic growth can also be defined in terms of more specific products of value, rather than just increased dollars. Thus, we could talk about the growth in real expenditures for education and health care as the two most important indicators of quality of life.

Economic growth refers to gross national income without deducting for costs. Such growth may be meaningless if the increase in costs is greater than the increase in income. Costs include war casualties, homicide casualties, and premature pollution deaths.

Statistics for change in national income, inflation, and population are relatively easy to obtain across places and time periods. Statistics on longevity as a measure of healthcare and years of schooling as a measure of education are also not so difficult. War, homicide, and pollution casualties may be more difficult, but reasonably obtainable.

II. CAUSES AND EFFECTS

Table 1 shows five effects of economic growth on the right, and five causes of economic growth on the left. The lower portion of the table emphasizes the upward-spiral effect of previous economic growth on subsequent economic growth. That occurs by way of such growth facilitators as (1) increased funding for growth, (2) growth policy that can occur without additional funding, (3) a multiplicity of government agencies working toward growth, and (4) a constitutional right to economic growth and lifetime learning. These causes, effects, and facilitators of economic growth will be discussed in further detail in this chapter.

Table 1. Causes, Effects, and Facilitators of Economic Growth

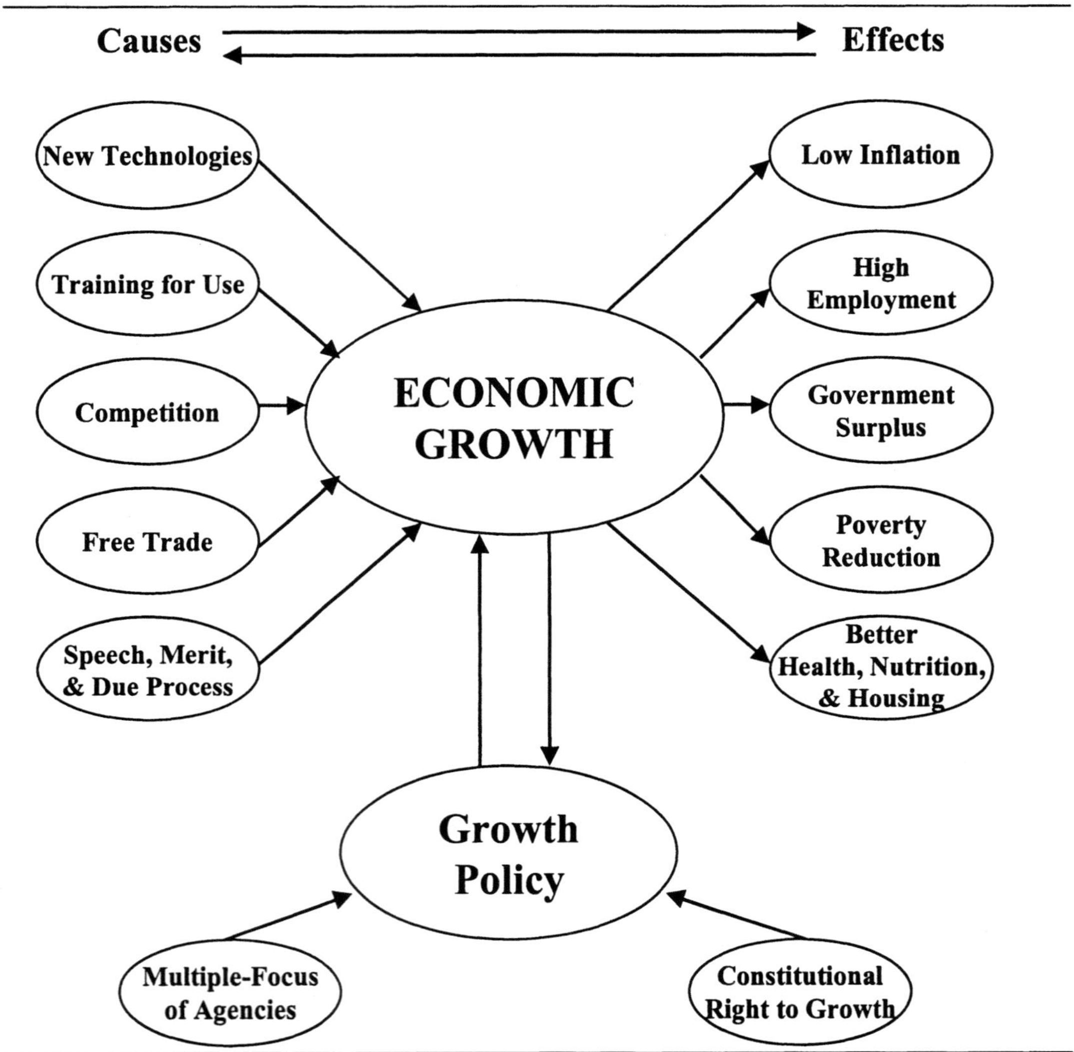

Notes:

1. All relations are positive. Thus there is no need for a plus sign on each arrow.
2. The first four causes on the left relate to technology, social, economic, and international policy respectively. The civil liberties combination of speech, merit, and due process is a combination of political, social, and legal policy.
3. The first four effects on the right are all economic. The combination of health, nutrition, and housing are generally included in part of science and technology policy.
4. The two facilitators below "Growth Policy" are political and legal.
5. The reason for mentioning how these causes, effects, and facilitators are related to the policy fields of economic, technology, social, political, international, and legal is because doing so brings out how economic growth depends on such a variety of policy fields and scholarly disciplines.

According to Table 1, there are five causes, five effects, and two growth policies. Most (but not all) of those 12 policies were discussed in "Win-Win Policy for Developing Nations" in the Autumn 2000 issue of *Developmental Policy.* For example, getting new technologies adopted is discussed in Table 2 and the accompanying text. Training for use is Table 3. Free trade regarding dollar exchange rates is Table 5. Table 4 discusses having multiple-focus agencies, and Table 6 talks about the constitutional right to growth. Table 1 deals with inflation and unemployment.

That only covers four of the five causes, two growth policies, and two of the five effects. The other causes and effects are discussed in the following places:

1. Competition is discussed in "Win-Win Economics" in the September 1999 issue of *Policy Evaluation.*
2. Free trade in terms of no tariffs on imports is discussed in "International Prosperity and Change" in the Spring 1997 issue of *Developmental Policy.*
3. Free speech, merit treatment, and fair procedure is discussed in "Win-Win Minority Rights" in the Spring 2001 issue of *Policy Evaluation.*
4. Having a government surplus is discussed in "Win-Win Economics" in the Summer 1999 issue of *Policy Evaluation.*
5. Poverty reduction is discussed in "Win-Win Poverty Reduction and Prevention" in the Spring 2000 issue of *Developmental Policy.*
6. Health care is Table 6 in "Win-Win Technology Policy" in the Autumn 1999 issue of *Developmental Policy.* Housing is Table 4 in the same article.
7. Nutrition and food policy are discussed in Table 2 and the text under "Food Prices" in the Spring 1996 issue of *Developmental Policy.*

III. How Table 1 Differs from Prior Presentations

Table 1 differs from the win-win productivity cycle presented in the Winter 1997 and the Spring 1999 *Developmental Policy.* The figure also appears on the book cover of *Developmental Policy* for 1999 and 2000. That productivity cycle figure is a four-stage flowchart, rather than a cause-and-effect arrow diagram. The causes represent the first stage in the cycle. Economic growth is the second stage. The effects are the third stage, and poverty reduction is the fourth. Table 1 substantially simplifies that more complicated win-win productivity cycle.

Table 1 also differs from what is shown on the cover of the summer issue of *Developmental Policy* in the following ways:

1. Table 1 adds free speech, merit treatment, and due process as important causes of economic growth.
2. Table 1 refers to better health, nutrition, and housing as an important composite effect.
3. Table 1 brings in poverty reduction as an effect separate from high employment. Poverty reduction may also require job facilitators, training programs, education equity, merit treatment, voting rights, and crime reduction–not just an expanding labor force.

4. Table 1 eliminates funding for growth as an effect. Including that variable leads to the false impression that lots of funding is needed in order to adopt the policy causes. That is not so. No substantial funding is needed in order to pass laws (1) requiring companies that sell electricity, transportation, and communication to rent their infrastructures at high rates to potential competitors, (2) lowering or removing tariffs on imports, (3) prohibiting interference with free speech, and (4) requiring merit treatment regardless of ethnic affiliation, gender, or other non-merit criteria. Minimum funding may be sufficient to get started in (5) encouraging businesses to adopt new technologies through tax avoidance and (6) encouraging individuals to obtain relevant training through conditional vouchers.

Chapter 11

WIN-WIN POVERTY REDUCTION AND PREVENTION

Win-win or super-optimizing analysis of public policy problems tries to find feasible solutions which can enable conservatives, liberals, and other major viewpoints to all come out ahead of their best initial expectations simultaneously. The elements in the analysis include (1) conservative goals and alternatives, (2) liberal goals and alternatives, (3) relations between the major alternatives and goals, (4) the development of win-win solutions, and (5) feasibility hurdles to overcome. The feasibility hurdles to be overcome include economic, administrative, political, psychological, legal, international, and technological hurdles, and the disruption of displaced firms and individuals.

As applied to social policy, we are especially talking about improving the quality of life of people at the bottom of the social hierarchy but to the benefit of all. This means public policy that relates to (1) employment and job facilitators, (2) education, financing, and integration, (3) merit treatment, (4) voting and political participation, and (5) crime reduction.

The Computer Revolution and contemporary globalization have the potential for generating great productivity and prosperity. They also have the potential for generating among so many people more unemployment and anger than the Industrial Revolution. This is so because so many poverty-generating displacement factors are operating simultaneously throughout the world. That includes productivity downsizing, free trade, defense conversion, and immigration. It also includes employing many groups of people who were not formerly competing so much for the available jobs, such as women, minorities, the disabled, and the elderly. A key object of an anti-poverty program should be to smooth the transition of displaced workers to other possibly better jobs, as well as to provide for the transition of the previously poor toward middle-class status.

Being poor in this context relates partly to individual income. It is, however, not possible to say that being poor means having less than a certain income or being below a certain income percentile in one's nation. One can live better at a low income in some places in the world than others. Being in the bottom 10 percentile in a wealthy nation may be better than being in the top 10 percentile in an impoverished nation. Poverty should be measured in terms of food, shelter, clothing, and medical care. A person or family is impoverished if they cannot afford (1) enough food to avoid all forms of malnutrition, (2) enough housing to not freeze in the winter time, (3) enough clothing to satisfy minimum cultural standards of dignity, and (4) enough medical care so that all members of the family have better than a 50% probability of living to age 60. The fourth point illustrates how our standards keep moving up since living to age 40 would have been considered good in medieval times, even by royalty.

Sometimes employment and education are included in the definition of poverty. Both employment and education are important for preventing poverty and for rising out of poverty, but they are not part of the definition. They are causes and to some extent effects of poverty. More important, they are policy variables subject to deliberate improvements through government decision-making.[1]

I. EMPLOYMENT (TABLE 1)

A. Conservative and Liberal Alternatives

Constrained public aid refers to restrictions on eligibility, benefit levels, income retention, and due process partly designed to deter applications for public aid. Generous public aid refers to broadness on those matters partly designed to provide more dignity to the poor.

The key issues on those four matters have been (1) allowing an impoverished family that has a father and mother present to receive aid, (2) providing for minimum benefit levels on a nationwide basis, (3) allowing recipients to keep a certain number of earned dollars per month, and (4) providing hearings in welfare disputes, including right to counsel.

B. Win-Win Alternatives

The SOS emphasis is away from arguing over those legal matters, and putting more emphasis on upgrading skills and providing job opportunities. Doing so may do more for decreasing poverty than a punitive deterrence approach and more for the dignity of the poor than a generous welfare approach.

Deterring poverty means making even more unpleasant the status of being poor so people will have more of an incentive to avoid being poor. Decreasing poverty means removing people from poverty by providing them with jobs or other income. Providing job opportunities may involve wage supplements to subsidize both potential employers into hiring welfare recipients and to subsidize recipients into accepting the jobs. The subsidy might also require employers to provide on-the-job training and recipients to pass the training course. On a higher level, it may be necessary for public policy to stimulate an expanding economy in order to create new jobs. Such stimulation might emphasize a pay roll tax that is refundable if the money is used for increasing productivity by way of new technologies, upgrading skills, or developing daycare centers.

---

[1] On win-win analysis, see William Baumol, *Superfairness: Applications and Theory* (MIT Press, 1986); Stuart Nagel, *Super-Optimum Solutions and Basic Concepts and Principles,* (Quorum Books, 1997); and Lawrence Susskind and Jeffrey Cruikshank, *Breaking the Impasse: Consensual Approaches to Resolving Public Disputes*, (Basic Books, 1987).

Table 1. Win-Win Analysis of Public Aid and Jobs

Criteria / Alternatives	C Deterrence of Poverty & Decrease Taxes	L Dignity of the Poor
C Constrained Public Aid	+	-
L Generous Public Aid	-	+
N Reformed Public Aid	0	0
SOS Job Facilitators 1. Contracting out Job Finding 2. Wage Vouchers 3. Training Vouchers 4. GNP Growth	++	++

As for employment of displaced workers or people in the culture of poverty, there are a number of job facilitators that have been shown to be reasonably effective, provided that the nation or community is willing to make a worthwhile investment. These job facilitators include:

1. Contracting out to employment services to find jobs for the unemployed on a commission basis. This means the job finder gets a substantial amount of money from the government after the worker has been on the job for six months. Such a commission arrangement provides the job finder with an incentive to determine the worker's aptitudes and interests so the worker will not quit or be fired before the commission is paid.
2. Wage vouchers that are given by the government to the unemployed to supplement what an employer can afford to pay. In return for being able to cash in the wage voucher, the employer must agree to hire unemployed people and provide them with on-the-job training. The worker must agree to perform the work and pass the training within six months when the vouchers end.
3. Vouchers can also be given for training that involves going to school, obtaining day care services, and moving to a new city. These voucher systems cost money. They may, however, soon more than pay for themselves if the workers get off some forms of public aid, pays taxes, and buys more goods and services with the multiplier effects that such buying has. Those employed workers may also refrain from anti-social activities and become better role models for their children and grandchildren.
4. The most important job facilitators are probably under the list of productivity causes such as national training, new technologies, competition, and free trade. They provide an expanding economy with more jobs widely available to displaced workers

and the chronically unemployed, regardless of the reasons for being displaced or unemployed.[2]

II. EDUCATION

A. Financing

The second item under poverty reduction and prevention is education. In this context, we are talking about elementary and secondary education, since adult training was already discussed. There are two big problems in providing better education for low-income children or children in families whose real incomes are falling contrary to general trends. The first problem is lack of money for the local schools. Low-income communities throughout the world are generally not able to raise sufficient local funds to provide adequate school buildings and teachers. There is a big need for more allocation of national or federal tax money to local education. It is not politically feasible to expect rich communities in a province to provide much support for the low-income communities. It is more politically feasible for the national government to do so.

The funding as of 1998 could come from channeling defense expenditures into local education expenditures. Defense expenditures are still at near Cold War levels in most countries, but there is no longer actual or potential warlike conflict between capitalism and communism. The high of the Cold War may have been when Russia was sending missiles to Cuba in the warlike early '60s. The U.S. defense budget is, however, now twice as high in the peacetime later '90s. Another advantage of federal funding is that the money could be used to provide differential salary incentives to teach in the impoverished schools. That is something local school boards have been unable to do because of the power over the local school boards by local unions and seniority teachers.

B. Integration (Table 2)

The second big problem in providing better education for low-income children is the need to bring those children into more contact with middle-class children who are above the poverty line, as defined in terms of food, shelter, clothing, medical care, or income. The Coleman Report of the 1960s found great variation across school districts in terms of probability of the average student going on to college or high school. Of the total variation, about 20% can be explained by differences in school facilities, 30% in terms of differences in salaries and experience of teachers, and 50% in terms of the middle-class nature of the interacting students. Having low-income students interact more with middle-income students means they are indirectly interacting with the middle-class parents of those students who

[2] On job facilitators, see Judith Gueron and Edward Pualy, *From Welfare to Work,* (Russell Sage, 1991); Demetra Nightingale and Robert Haveman, *The Work Alternative: Welfare Reform and the Realities of the Job Market,* (The Urban Institute, 1995); and World Development Indicators, *World Development Report 1995: Workers in an Integrating World,* (Oxford, 1995).

encourage their children to think in terms of getting more education and qualifying for middle-class occupations.

One of the best ways of promoting that kind of interaction is through housing vouchers, rather than school vouchers. The housing voucher enables the low-income family to move up one concentric circle in the city in which they live, or to move from an impoverished rural area to a livable urban area. Doing so increases the interclass interaction to the benefit of the low-income children without pulling down the middle-class children, so long as they are not overwhelmed. Middle-class families can also be encouraged to move into low-income areas that are close to urban employment by being sold condominium housing in sheltered communities. The developers of such communities (who receive free government land) are required to set aside about 25% of the condos for low-income families, and all children attend the same community public school.

Table 2: School Integration

Criteria **Alternatives**	**C** **Save Taxes & Minimize Disruption**	**L** **Improve Education**
C No Government-Imposed Racial Integration	+	-
L Government-Imposed Integration, Especially Busing	-	+
N Some Busing for Racial Integration, or Upgrade low income schools	0	0
SOS 1. Economic Integration 2. Line Drawing 3. Housing 4. Community Development	++	++

When it comes to elementary and high school integration, conservatives want a minimum of government-imposed integration. This can be justified on the grounds that it saves taxes and it minimizes disruption.

Liberals advocate government-imposed racial integration, especially by busing black students to white schools, although it may be too politically unpopular to bus white students to black schools. Some black schools can be converted to experimental magnet schools or to non-schools. The remaining black schools can be upgraded through programs of special funding for better facilities and teachers. This can be justified on the grounds that it improves inner-city education for the benefit of the total society. The neutral position would be some busing and some upgrading, but not as much as is advocated by liberals.

An SOS alternative might involve emphasizing economic-class integration, rather than racial integration. This may be especially important in cities where a high percentage of the public school students are black or minority, but they vary in terms of family income and economic class background. This may also be important because the ambition level of poor kids gets raised by contact with middle-class kids, whereas neither black nor white kids benefit from contact with each other if they are all from the same economic class.

Economic integration can partly occur by redrawing the lines of the neighborhood schools so as to provide a better economic mix for each school. Housing vouchers to enable poor families to move to more middle class schools are also relevant. Some busing can also be used but with more reliance on line drawing.

The results would be to save more tax money and have less disruption than a program that relies more on racial integration and busing. Also the SOS alternative might do more for improving education in terms of changing peer groups across class lines than busing for racial integration.[3]

III. MERIT TREATMENT (TABLE 3)

The third item under poverty reduction and prevention is merit treatment. It refers to the fact that poverty is frequently based on discrimination that relates to race, religion, or ancestral nationality. Merit treatment does not refer to giving preferences to redress past discrimination. It refers here to treating people on the basis of their individual merit, with an outreach training program for those who are potentially well-qualified, but who cannot meet high reasonable standards of employment or college admission. More specifically this kind of outreach training means that applicants with low-income backgrounds who almost pass qualifying tests are invited to participate in a semester-long training program to better prepare them for the test, the job, or the education. Low-income in this context means that their elementary and secondary schools had per capita expenditures substantially below the national average. If they fail to qualify after the training program, then they are channeled elsewhere. Such an outreach training program increases the actual merit of those with high potential that has not probably been adequately nurtured, as indicated by the objective criterion of the per capita education expenditures.

[3] On education, see Jean Anyon, *Ghetto Schooling: A Political Economy of Urban Educational Reform*, (Columbia University, 1997); Centre for Educational Research and Innovation, *Adult Illiteracy and Economic Performance*, (OECD, 1992); and Nelly Stromquist, *Education in Urban Areas: Cross-National Dimensions*, (Praeger, 1994).

Table 3: Equal Employment Opportunity

Goals Alternatives	C Productivity of Work Force	L Equity or Fairness in Distributing Benefits
C Merit Hiring	+	-
L Preferential Hiring	-	+
N Seeking Qualified Minorities	0	0
SOS OR WIN-WIN Upgrade Skills	++	++

A. Conservative and Liberal Positions

With regard to race relations, the key conservative goal seems to be to judge people in accordance with merit. In the past, conservatives offered a variety of justifications for racism. That is no longer the case. Merit treatment is now the rule, and in that context they talk about color-blind hiring and color-blind admissions, in which no preferences are given for being black, female, or any kind or minority.

Liberals on the other hand, talk about the need for diversity, equity, and better distribution, and in order to achieve it, they feel quota systems should be abolished. A quota system implies accepting a certain number of black applicants for a job, or for a law school, regardless of qualifications. What liberals feel is that there should be preferences given, but only in cases where a white person and a black person are equally well qualified. More extreme liberals might even admit the black person when the white person is only slightly better qualified. That is how the preference system can be used in order to achieve diversity.

B. A Win-Win Alternative

A win-win alternative would be capable of achieving high merit, high diversity, fair-ness, and equity simultaneously. How might that be brought about? One alternative that makes a lot of sense is outreach training. Outreach training does not involve giving any preferences to people who apply, for instance, to law school or to work in a management capacity at GM, but instead, if they have potential, they will be admitted into the program. In many cases they will have gone to an elementary school or high school in an area where the amount of money spent per student is below the amount spent across the country. In other words, they meet three criteria of (1) they cannot qualify on the basis of their present scores, (2) they have a lot of potential, and (3) they had an economically disadvantaged elementary or high school education.

If they meet those criteria, then before entering law school they would be tutored on what is involved in doing well on the law school admission test, similar to a Kaplan or Princeton Review prep course for people that do not have the money available. They would not only be tutored for the law school admission test, but are also trained towards what is involved in being a good law student. They get college credit for passing these courses. If they fail a course, they are dropped from the program. This is not a gift, it has to be earned. After taking the prep course, if they still do not get a high enough grade on the LSAT, then they are also disqualified. They get no preferences or points, but get the credits and grades for the summer course which can help bring their grade point average up to a minimum threshold for admission. A similar outreach training program has been used for years by West Point, Annapolis, and the Air Force Academy to work with various minorities to bring them to a level where they could be admitted without any kind of preferences at all. It does cost money, but it is worthwhile, because if the military provides diversity among officers, it may be very helpful with regard to improving morale among the troops, many of whom come from various minorities.

Unfortunately, the current Congress has voted to almost completely wipe out the outreach training programs of the military academies. It's rather short-sighted, but if something involves spending money for human resources training, the payoff is not immediate, and Congress may be reluctant to put forth the money. Congress is very sensitive about producing results to show the American public before the next election, which is never far away. One might say, "What can be done to provide for more foresight on the part of American politicians?" One plan that might be tried is the establishment of something similar to the Japanese Ministry of International Trade and Industry that consists of three representatives from industry, three from labor, and three from government. The government officials are not even directly elected. The President, or Prime Minister, appoints the government officials, and they are given money to invest in various kinds of programs, such as outreach training programs, the training of displaced workers, or investing in new technologies. They can do this with a better time horizon than members of Congress, who are only serving for two year terms. The member of congress would have supervision over the new ministry. Such an organization, being non-governmental, could be associated with the department of education.

The feasibility problem of outreach training is an economic one. It costs money. It costs money for the training, and the payoff may not be seen for a while. For instance, the training of minorities in a special summer program for law school may not pay off until after they graduate and become better role models and provide better legal service to people in the minority community. Unfortunately, economic feasibility may require as we've mentioned, institutions such as Congress having a longer time horizon than they presently do.[4]

[4] On merit treatment, see Sheldon Danziger and Peter Gottschalk, *America Unequal*, (Harvard, 1995); Ted Gurr, *Minorities at Risk: A Global View of Ethnopolitical Conflicts*, (Institute of Peace, 1993); and Barbara Nelson and Najma Chowdhury, *Women and Politics Worldwide*, (Yale, 1994).

IV. VOTING (TABLE 4)

As for the voting item, that refers to the fact that low-income people need to be empowered to shift more for themselves and be less dependent on public-aid systems. Both conservatives and liberals use concepts like empowerment and power to the people. Conservatives sometimes use such concepts in an overly paternalistic way. Liberals sometimes use such concepts in an unnecessarily frightening revolutionary way. Both sides are likely to agree that enfranchising poor people (at least in theory) is a good thing for society and especially democracy. In the context of voting, that means making it easier for qualified low-income-people to vote as a minimum form of political participation. They are frequently in effect disenfranchised because they find it more difficult to register at the time of voting, as is done in some countries and states. Low-income people also find it difficult to lose time from work in order to vote. A simple solution is to make election day a holiday as some countries do, or at least to hold major elections on Sunday or on multiple days. One should also be allowed to vote at one's home precinct, workplace, precinct, or any precinct, so long as one passes the test of not having previously been exposed to a container of invisible ink while voting. If more low-income people participate in politics and voting, then more public policies would be adopted that relate to the kind of job facilitators, education, and merit treatment discussed above.

Table 4: Voting Registration and Turnout

Criteria **Alternatives**	**C** **No Double Voting**	**L** **Universal Adult Voting**
C Leave As Is	+	-
L Postcard Registration or Tinker with Motor Voter	-	+
N Precinct Registration, Permanent Registration	0	0
SOS 1. On Site Same Day, or Census Registration 2. Vote Anywhere 3. Extended Times 4. Invisible Ink	++	++

A. Conservative and Liberal Positions

There the US does not look good relative to the rest of the world when it comes to voter turnout. We have roughly (these are very round numbers) two hundred million adults, of which approximately half are registered to vote. But, only about half of those registered to vote actually do. That's about 50 million. That means if just 26 million out of the 50 million vote for a certain candidate for president, he gets in. This can be a landslide if each state is hotly contested, even though it's only 36 million out of 200 million possible voters. It's not so good when, in effect, twelve percent of the population can decide who will sit in the Oval office. We are not undemocratic in the sense of prohibiting people, but less democratic than we should be in the sense of facilitating voter turnout.

The true conservative goal might be to promote the election of conservative candidates but they are not going to say that. What they actually say is that they want to avoid multiple voting. They do not want any schemes that will allow cheating at the polls. Liberals on the other hand, are very concerned about people who do not vote, so they want to decrease non-voting by adults who could be eligible. The conservative position promotes a decrease in multiple voting a number of ways. One of the most extreme positions is to purge the voter rolls every ten years and make people register over again. This would guard against individuals still being present on the voter rolls who have moved or died. It greatly decreases the number of people who register if you have to do it over and over again. Having advanced registration may make a difference with regard to decreasing multiple voting, but it also decreases voting in general. Liberals also want advanced registration, but they want to make the process easier. They support ideas like post card registration, or registration at the time you get your driver's license -so called motor-vehicle legislation. They also support keeping the polls open a few hours later to make it easier to vote on election day, Unfortunately, the liberal solutions in total wouldn't make much of a difference, as more fundamental change is necessary.

B. A Win-Win Alternative

What really needs to be adopted is the kind of system presently being used in many countries of the world, including, Canada, South Africa, Mexico, and Mozambique, and states such as Wisconsin and Minnesota. It involves a few innovations. First of all, there is no requirement of advance registration. You can register in advance if you want to, but you can also register on-site the day of election. Many people who don't vote on election day through on-site registration, that would no longer be a problem. Also, if elections were to be moved to a non-working day instead of a Tuesday, more people would be able to participate. In Catholic countries like Italy, France, and Mexico, election day is on a Sunday, when people don't work. Other nations string their elections over a couple of days. Another improvement would allow people to vote in either their home precinct or their work precinct, or to even allow them to vote in any precinct, provided there is some way of checking to make sure they haven't voted in another. Multiple-precinct voting can make a large difference in voter turnout.

With all these facilitators, however, the conservative problem of multiple voting rises again. The way that problem is solved in South Africa, Mexico, Mozambique, and other countries, is by having voters dip their hand into a bowl of invisible ink. If you show up at a polling place anytime in the day after that, including your original polling place, your hand is viewed under an ultraviolet lamp, and if it shows that you have already voted, you are denied the right to vote again, and can possibly be arrested. The invisible ink method works much better than asking people to sign their names, because names can be forged much more easily than hands. It is a good example of a win-win solution because it would substantially decrease multiple voting and substantially decrease non-voting. It helps to achieve both kinds of goals simultaneously, like the previously mentioned outreach training, or the more profitable and cleaner processes that relate to environmental protection and economic growth. All four that we have discussed so far are capable of achieving the conservative and liberal goal more successfully than either the conservative or liberal alternative.

On-site registration, the non-working election day, multiple precincts, and the invisible ink method all have a political feasibility problem. This problem is political in the sense that it is very difficult to get such a measure through Congress or through a state legislature. This is because one political party is likely to have enough strength to block it, namely the party which thinks it will suffer as a result of expanded voter turnout. As long as it has enough power to stop these measures, they will never be adopted. If, however, they ever were adopted, they are not likely to be repealed. There is a kind of ratchet effect on new facilitators once they are adopted, because the party in power will look bad if it decreases the ability of people to register and vote. These measures are likely to be adopted when the Democrats have enough influence in the Congress or in the various state legislatures. The traditional thinking is that the Democratic party benefits more from expanded voter registration and turnout than the Republican party, due to the fact that a higher percentage of non-voters consist of the people who are poorer and less educated than average. Such voters are more likely to vote Democratic. The problem is political, but it may only be a temporary problem, as hopefully all the other feasibility problems may be temporary.[5]

V. CRIME REDUCTION (TABLE 5)

The fifth item under poverty reduction and prevention relates to crime. Being poor may be a key factor in engaging in street crimes like mugging and burglary, as contrasted to middle-class crimes like embezzlement and swindling. Here we are concerned not with how poverty causes crime, but rather with how crime causes poverty, especially drug-related criminal activity. As with the other four anti-poverty policy variables, we are talking about how anti-crime improvements can be made that will result in poverty reduction and prevention. A big factor in inner-city poverty in cities throughout the world (especially the United States) is the highly negative influence on productivity of drugs like derivatives of opium and cocaine. The availability of such drugs can turn a potentially productive person into a drug addict, or worse into a drug dealer who creates other drug addicts.

[5] On voting, see Yogesh Atal and Else Oyen, *Poverty and Participation in Civil Society,* (UNESCO, 1997); John Friedmann, *Empowerment: Politics of Alternative Development,* (Blackwell, 1992); and Frances Piven Richard Cloward, *Why Americans Don't Vote,* (Pantheon, 1988).

Table 5: Dealing With the Drug Problem

Criteria Alternatives	C Decrease Crime Committing, Reduce Drug Dealing	L Societal Productivity Avoid Adverse Side Effects of Enforcement
C Law Enforcement Crackdown	+	-
L Legalization	-	+
N Treatment & Education Prohibit Coke & Heroin, Not Pot	0	0
SOS Medicalization to De-Profitize Drug Sales	++	++

One solution might be to medicalize the drug problem. That means drug addicts are considered sick people, rather than criminals guilty of possession or sale to get money to buy drugs. That further means such addicts would be treated under whatever national healthcare exists by being given a phase-out prescription that gets lower in dosage each month. If they stay on prescription opium or cocaine forever like diabetics stay on insulin, this is still an improvement over the criminal drug market in multiple ways:

1. One improvement is that drug dealers would have no incentives to give low-income 10-year olds free samples, because they would be just creating patients for the healthcare service, not new paying customers.
2. Another improvement is that almost 70% of all the muggings and burglaries would end, since that is the percent of muggings and burglaries that are committed by drug addicts seeking money to buy drugs.
3. Likewise, almost 70% of the murders in the U.S. and some other countries are drug-related, meaning they are committed by drug dealers fighting for control, or committed by addicts in a bungled mugging or burglary.
4. Another benefit especially to some developing countries would be lessening of the corruption of police and government officials by wealthy drug dealers.
5. A further benefit is the tremendous saving in prison costs, court costs, police costs, and other costs that are part of the criminalizing of drug addiction, as contrasted to the relatively low cost involved in medicalizing drug addiction and the high benefits mentioned above.

A. Conservative and Liberal Positions

The last policy problem regards drug-related crime, which has become an increasingly serious issue. It currently consumes a great deal of money in the US, and is causing enormous losses in productivity. It is causing governments to engage in corruption and police officers to use abuse behavior due to the tremendous frustration brought on by the drug war.

The key conservative goal in this context is to eliminate or greatly reduce drug-dealing. This means reducing the buying and selling of illegal drugs, most commonly heroin, cocaine, and marijuana. Cocaine and crack represent the largest problem, as they are involved in a large percentage that occurs. Sixty to seventy percent of all people who are arrested for crimes against poverty or crimes against persons are arrested under circumstances that indicate that they are stealing in order to get money for drugs. Often, they are under the influence of drugs while committing crimes. The crimes against the persons usually involve power plays for staking out drug territory. They frequently lead to murder, because under the influence of drugs, people behave in a more aggressive way than they would otherwise.

Liberals are especially concerned about reducing the side-effects of the war on drugs. These side-effects refer to the police engaging in more illegal arrests, illegal searches, and illegal interrogations than before crack cocaine became very widespread in the mid-80's. They also include the tremendous amount of money necessary for the imprisonment of over 1,000,000 people in our prisons and 500,000 people in our jails. That money could be much better spent on health care, education, or other more useful purposes.

The conservative solution has been to try to repress the sale and possession of drugs. This law enforcement type of approach is an approach of repression, of prohibition. One of the more extreme liberal approaches, although becoming somewhat more popular, is legalization. The policy of drug prohibition and repression is analogous to the policy of liquor prohibition. Back then, the U.S. realized that liquor prohibition didn't work, and that the policy's abolishment was better, even if that means more alcohol related crime. Legalization is the more liberal alternative to conservative police enforcement and repression.

B. A Win-Win Alternative

The object of the win-win solution is to come up with some kind of idea that wipes out the drug dealers, but will not increase the use of drugs. Another way to phrase it is to de-profitize drug dealing. If you de-profitize drug dealing, then you would also eliminate the side effects. Then organized crime would decrease accordingly. Another side effect which would be eliminated is the corruption of government officials due to the availability of "mutually profitable arrangements" with large dealers. An ounce of pure cocaine has street value higher than that of an ounce of gold. This causes a lot of frustration for the police, because as soon as one drug-dealer gets arrested and imprisoned or killed, there is another set up to immediately to take their place. The money is just too good for some people to turn down.

The way to de-profitize drug dealing is to treat drug addicts like sick people, and to consider them criminals only if they engage in crimes other than possession and use of drugs. A key part of the treatment is to treat drug addicts as being in need of medical treatment under our current health care programs. As health care plans move in the direction of becoming universal, the need to cover drug addiction is important. If drug addicts are considered to be sick people and eligible for prescription drugs, that could include a cocaine substitute or even actual cocaine under a cocaine maintenance program. The profits of drug dealing would be wiped out because addicts would be able to get what they need through their subsidized HMO. These maintenance prescriptions would usually be given on a long-term, phase-out basis until the person is clean. If they never kick their drug habit, their doctors will be able to prescribe additional doses. No more would drug dealers be interested in hooking ten-year-old kids with free samples; all they'd be doing is creating new patients for the HMOs. The dealers would eventually be forced to look for some alternative occupation as did the bootleg liquor dealers of the past. At the present time, anything would be better than drug dealing, for society and for the lives of drug dealers and crack users.

The win-win solution is plagued by psychological feasibility problems. Many don't believe that such availability will have any effect other than to increase the use of drugs. The idea that people who are not drug addicts are going to go to their HMO and say "I'm a drug addict, I'm on cocaine," when they want to experiment is farfetched. Such a declaration would likely cause them to sacrifice many opportunities that they might otherwise have. Employers are not too enthusiastic about hiring drug addicts. The real drug addicts, though, do have an incentive to go to the HMOs. There they can get a maintenance prescription without having to rob or kill for it, and without having to run the risk of getting arrested or killed themselves.

This kind of approach appeals to some libertarian conservatives who think that a repression program involves more problematic government interference than interference in the economy. It should also appeal to liberals. It's better than legalization because legalization means that controls would be much less strict, and that anybody could have access to drugs, including children. Those children would likely grow up to be much less productive members of society. Legalization, in fact, would have a very bad effect on national productivity, whereas this kind of program, which is only for confirmed drug addicts, would have few new effects. They are not going to be a whole lot of new drug addicts created because there will not be a set of drug-dealers encouraging the younger generation to become drug addicts.

As said before, the feasibility problem here is psychological. People are resistant to the idea of giving drugs to anyone, let alone those who are already addicts. That sounds somehow evil, but it's less evil than the present system might be. Because this plan is psychologically hard to accept, it is very difficult politically to adopt. Economically, this solution would cost far less than what is currently being done. Cocaine, for instance, is very cheap to produce. Its high price largely has to do with police repression, which causes the costs of drug dealing to rise, and therefore the street price to rise also. There might also be some feasibility problems with regard to administering such a program. The drugs possessed by HMOs and hospitals must be carefully monitored so that they don't fall into the wrong hands. This can be taken care of by authorizing only one doctor in the whole HMO to prescribe drug maintenance programs or drugs. This would greatly decrease the amount of people with access, and would thereby decrease the risk. Also, in order to be eligible to receive a drug maintenance prescription, a person must be a confirmed addict. This would require testing, over time, of the levels of drugs in a person's system to see if they qualify. The administrative part of the program should not necessarily require people to accept a phase-out arrangement. Such restrictions would cause people to avoid the program, and would cause the formation of a black market, which defeats the entire purpose. That is why a similar program did not succeed in England. As long as these people are treated as sick people, not criminals, this kind of administration is likely to succeed.[6]

VI. The "Widening" U.S. Inequality Gap?

The September 5, 1999 issue of the *New York Times* at page 14 has an article entitled, "The Gap Between the Rich and Poor Found Substantially Wider." The data comes from the Congressional Budget Office. Like some other headlines in this field, this headline is a bit of a misinterpretation of reality in the following ways:

1. The *NYT* article deals with the United States and not with the world in general, as the *DEV News* article referred to above does. The *DEV News* article emphasizes that changes in the equality gap depend on whether we are talking about (1) wealthy countries like the USA, (2) poor countries like those in Africa, or (3) middle countries in Asia.
2. The *NYT* article deals with changes in the 22-year-period between 1977 and 1999 and not the longer perspective of the *DEV News* article.
3. The *NYT* article talks about the lowest one-fifth getting poorer, and the highest one-fifth getting richer. The more categories one uses, the more one can show the rich getting richer, and the poorer getting poorer. This might be especially true if we compare the bottom 1% with the top 1%, which means 100 categories. This is much less true if one compares the bottom half with the top half and maybe even untrue over a longer time span or among most non-U.S. countries.
4. The *NYT* article talks only in terms of income. It leaves out the fact that the health care gap (as measured by longevity) may be getting smaller.
5. The *NYT* article also leaves out that the education gap (as measured by years of schooling) may be getting smaller.
6. The *NYT* article also leaves out the substantial improvements in equal opportunity as a result of reduction in discrimination against women, minorities, the aged, disabled, rural people, poor people, and other non-merit discrimination.
7. The *NYT* article just talks about the inequality gap getting wider, and not about the poor getting richer even though the inequality gap is getting wider. By richer, we mean in this context dollar income as contrasted to health, education, and equality of opportunity. Buried in the article, however, is the statement that "Since 1993, the economy has lifted the incomes of all of the income groups tracked by the budget office" which is almost contrary to the headlines.
8. Talking in terms of the half-empty versus the half-full bottle and how can one give almost diametrically opposed spin to the same data, one should note that the *NYT* article says, "The richest 2.7 million people and the hundred million at the other end of the scale will each have about $620 billion to spend." The *NYT* reporter indicates

---

[6] On crime, see Nicholas Dorn, Jorgen Jepsen, and Ernesto Savona, *European Drug Policies and Enforcement,* (St. Martins, 1996); Samuel Walker, *Sense and Nonsense about Crime: A Policy Guide*, (Brooks/Cole, 1989); and Franklin Zimring and Gordon Hawkins, *The Search for Rational Drug Control,* (Cambridge, 1992).

> this is terrible that 100 million people have only the same amount of money to spend as just 2.7 million people have. What the reporter fails to explicitly or implicitly say is that $620 billion divided by a hundred million "poor" people at the bottom on the economic ladder means $6,200 per person. That means $24,800 for a family of four. In other words, the hundred million poorest people in the United States have a fantastic per capita income as measured by UN standards which say that the international poverty line is $1,460 for a family of four per year or $365 per person or a dollar a day. Even for wealthy countries like the United States, the UN defines relative poverty as $14.40 per day per person or $5,256 a year per person or $21,024 for a family of four. The $24, 800 for a family of four in the bottom 100 million of the U.S. is also not inflated by averaging rich people with the poor people. These bottom 100 million are all relatively "poor" if we consider the rich to be the top 1% or 2.7 million, as the article does, and the middle class to be the middle 168 million.

Liberals who are interested in reducing the inequality gap may tend to exaggerate how it is getting worse. That does not necessarily arouse the public to want to reduce the inequality gap. It may cause the public to think (1) a widening inequality gap is inevitable, (2) a widening gap is desirable because during the time period between 1977 and 1999, most middle class people improved their quality of life when the gap was supposedly widening, and (3) this plays into the hands of those who say the poor will always be with us and there is nothing we can do about it.

Pointing out the progress that has been made can be more inspirational to make further progress, whereas emphasizing the progress that has not been made can be demoralizing although some people may react in opposite ways. Emphasizing lack of progress or policy problems in general can be demoralizing to those who give up easily, but inspirational to those who welcome challenges. Likewise emphasizing progress can cause complacency among those who are easily satisfied, but be inspirational to those who like to be on an upward roll.

Good policy studies describes progress or the lack of it realistically, emphasizing relevant conditions. Good policy studies also emphasizes how further progress can be made, regardless whether there has been big or little progress in the recent past, assuming that major conservative and liberal goals on the issues have not yet been met.

Chapter 12

THE ALLEGED DOWNSIDE OF ECONOMIC GROWTH

World Bank Book is called the Quality of Growth. This is an attempt to get at the downside of economic growth. I would say it mainly consists of displaced workers and firms. Others would say it consists of pollution, crime, loss of religious values. All three are untrue.

I. POLLUTION

On the matter of pollution, economic growth mainly means new technologies. Without them, there is not likely to be much economic growth. New technologies includes those which are more profitable and cleaner, thereby lessening and not increasing pollution. The best examples are:

1. In *agriculture* we now have genetically modified corn, soybeans, etc., which means less pesticides, herbicides, artificial fertilizer or any farm products which cause pollution.
2. In *transportation*, we are moving toward vehicles that can run on hybrid energy, which is half oil and half electricity. Also imminent are vehicles that can run on hydrogen or helium fusion, and vehicles made out of polymers that get twice the mileage per gallon due to their light weight and great strength.
3. In the realm of *manufacturing* we have new processes that are more profitable and cheaper, such as processing soybeans and processing minerals to separate out the pure gold or copper.
4. *Energy* forms are moving away from expensive and disappearing oil. We long ago moved away from dirty coal. We are moving more toward second generation safe nuclear, massive solar, hydrogen and helium fusion at the manufacturing level.

II. Crime

On the matter of crime, it is utter nonsense to say that economic growth increases crime. It may indeed have short disruptive effects by displacing workers who may then resort to crime to replace wages. Rural people driven off the land by mechanization may become criminals in city slums and shanty towns. However,

1. Economic growth means increased societal income, increased societal spending, and thus more jobs with higher income thereby decreasing criminal behavior.
2. Crimes are especially prevalent in times of recession and unemployment which is the opposite of economic growth. They are also prevalent in times of severe inflation when the income of people only buys half of what it bought before, so they resort to crime. Economic growth is also the opposite of inflation. Inflation occurs when too many dollars chase too few goods. Economic growth means lots more goods, thus decreasing crime causing inflation.

III. Loss of Religious Values

On the matter of religious values, it may also be nonsense to say they conflict with economic growth. There is no question that increasing new technologies along with the sciences that lead to economic growth does decrease superstition and more ignorance-based theologies, but what about ethical social values?. Do they decrease? The answer is overwhelmingly the opposite. Why is that? The answer is simply that in time of scarce resources people treat each other like concentration camp inmates, fighting over those scarce resources. The golden rule goes out the window. When a developing nation consists of 60 percent of its population earning less than one dollar a day, how can one expect people who are starving and watching their children starve to be nice to other families? It is almost the law of the jungle for two-thirds of the world living in utter poverty, with about one-third, or two billion people, earning less that one dollar per day, and another one-third earning less than two dollars per day. Even in the sliver of six billion people on earth who live in the richest country in the world, the United States, there are significant numbers of impoverished people who are on drugs and who will rob and kill to get money to buy cocaine.

When economic growth comes to impoverished countries or to rich countries with impoverished segments, then people's values become more other directed rather than less. Their other directed values are not based on a fear of going to hell, which is hard to justify by modern science. Their other directed values are based on being well enough off that they can afford to have other directed values. Thus economic growth increases golden rule values although they may not be religion-based. Presumably, religious ministers are more interested in people following the golden rule even if they do so for secular reasons, than ministers are in having people be highly religious in a superstitious way, as is often the case in developing nations or in America's ghettos, where they rob and kill to feed their families or to buy drugs.

FISHING VERSUS TEACHING HOW TO DECIDE

The Peace Corps for years has had a motto or slogan that says, "Give a person a fish and they will eat for a day. Teach a person how to fish, and they will eat for life."

Perhaps the Peace Corps should be renamed The Peace, Prosperity, and Democracy Corps in order to give it a broader mandate.

Its new motto might then be, "Give a country peace, prosperity, and democracy, and it will then have those three desirable goals for at least a short time. Teach a country how to do systematic policy evaluation (or better yet, how to do win-win analysis) and it may have peace, prosperity, and democracy for at least a generation."

Chapter 13

OVERCOMING THE CAN'T-DO LIST

I. THE LIST

The following list represents points that are frequently made by people in both developing and industrial countries to explain why they are not doing better on the key UN development indicators of per capita income, average length of life, and average education level achieved. There is room for improvement in all countries. Likewise, all countries have cynics, skeptics, negativists, and other such people who emphasize the can't-do aspects of development rather than the can-do aspects.

The can't-do list is arranged in pairs because some cynics frequently say the country cannot develop because it has too little X, and other cynics say it cannot develop because it has too much X. Thus, it can only develop for such cynical thinking if it has exactly the midpoint on X--whatever that is.

These pairs of can't-do ideas nicely lend themselves to a kind of win-win analysis. Some people say that development is hampered by having too much X, and others say it is hampered by having too much Y, where X and Y seem to be opposites. Win-win analysis tries to find ways that one can have X and Y simultaneously, or better yet, have the good effects of X and the good effects of Y simultaneously.

For example, on the first pair, lack of technology is a problem in all countries. The problem can be lessened by providing private sector businesses with public policy incentives to adopt new technologies. Such incentives might include a 3% payroll tax that is completely refundable if the money is used to adopt new technologies.

Likewise, on the second half of that first pair, technology downsizing is an undesirable problem because it results in workers and firms becoming unemployed when they may be well qualified for other jobs. Public policy can facilitate their getting into those other jobs by providing for (1) training vouchers, (2) moving and commuting allowances, (3) temporary wage subsidies, (4) commissions to placement agencies that are paid only after a worker has been on the job for at least six months, and (5) policies to promote economic growth, which creates new jobs.

1. **Economic**
   a. Wealth
      (1) Lack of money.
      (2) Evil influence of the rich.
   b. Risk Taking
      (1) Fear of unforeseen expenses.
      (2) Unwillingness to take risks.
   c. Inequality Gap
      (1) If per capita income goes up, then inequality will be greater.
      (2) We need more inequality to have role model incentives rather than have everybody be equally poor.
   d. Class Differences
      (1) The caste or class system interferes with merit treatment.
      (2) Class differences are needed for incentives to be more productive and income earning.
   e. Corporations
      (1) Multinational corporations are evil.
      (2) Big corporations are capable of benefiting from economies of large-scale operation.
2. **Technology**
   a. Technology
      (1) Lack of technology.
      (2) Technology downsizing.
   b. World Resources
      (1) Developing nations do not have their share of the world's resources.
      (2) If developing nations did have their share, the world would collapse.
   c. Food
      (1) To much starvation.
      (2) We must not eat food that has insecticides, herbicides, artificial fertilizer, or genetic modification.
3. **Social**
   a. Education
      (1) Lack of education.
      (2) Too many overeducated people.
   b. What Has Been Already Done
      (1) We already did X and that's enough.
      (2) Doing X is trivial, and obviously not enough, but our people are too easily satisfied.
   c. Progress Being Made
      (1) Things are getting better by themselves, so why work at it?
      (2) Things are getting worse by themselves, but our people are unwilling to work at it.
   d. Speaking English
      (1) Our people cannot speak English to learn the world's technologies.
      (2) Our people need to speak their native languages to have self-esteem.
   e. Religious Influence

(1) Religious traditionalism holds back progress.
(2) Decreasing religion causes people to be exploitative.

f. Population Size
(1) Population too big to feed.
(2) Population too small to bargain for lower food prices when importing.

4. Political

a. Party Systems
(1) Confusion of multi-party system.
(2) Lack of diversity of two-party system.

b. Regionalism
(1) Divisive regionalism.
(2) Lack of regional autonomy.

5. International

Comparisons With Other Places
(1) Other places are worse, so we should not be concerned.
(2) Other places are so much better that it looks hopeless.

6. Legal

Corruption
(1) Too much corruption.
(2) Our businesses are not internationally competitive because they don't know how to offer bribes.

II. Six Can't-Do Points Made by Officials from the India Institute of Public Administration

The PSO Coordinator recently did a set of policy analysis workshops at the India Institute of Public Administration in New Delhi. The Institute trains high-level civil servants for policymaking activities. It is to the Institute's credit that they are open to new ideas like win-win analysis. It is not, however, to the Institute's credit that the Institute seems to be run by people who seem to have a rather strong can't-do attitude for a country that especially needs a can-do attitude.

It especially needs such an attitude because it is the biggest country in the world in terms of population that has so much violent friction between (1) Hindus and Moslems, (2) males and females, especially females who do not have sufficient dowries or fail to give birth to sons, (3) rich and poor, especially members of the untouchable caste, (4) Indians and Pakistanis, and (5) Fundamentalist Hindus and more secular Hindus. It also needs a can-do attitude because (1) the per capita income is so low, (2) the average length of life is so low as a measure of health, and (3) the literacy level is so low as a measure of education. That covers peace and prosperity. India may not even do so well on democracy with regard to allowing the people in the provinces to choose their own governors and legislatures without a veto from the central government.

The following points were actually made by the people who head the India Institute of Public Administration in seeking to justify the above conditions, especially the poverty conditions.

1. The world's resources would be exhausted if India's per capita income went up from substantially less than $1,000 per person up to $1,000, especially oil resources.
   (This fails to recognize that the oil resources will probably be exhausted by the middle of the 21st century, regardless of what happens in India. But, human ingenuity is already planning alternative energy sources such as nuclear fusion based on the hydrogen in water or the helium that can be mined from the moon, or massive solar energy from a rotating magnifying glass in the sky, and from more efficient solar storage batteries.)
2. It is not so desirable to have great policy thinkers because they frequently go bad in their later years. The example given is Mikhail Gorbachev who succeeded in dismantling the Soviet dictatorship, but did not succeed in getting elected to office in the new government.
   (Nearly all the great policymakers in history were considered great because they did not retreat in the sense of becoming evil such as American and world renowned greats like Woodrow Wilson and Franklin Roosevelt.)
3. India has no major leaders since Gandhi and Nehru, but neither does the rest of the world.
   (Every developing region has had major leaders since 1945, such as Mikhail Gorbachev from East Europe, Nelson Mandela from Africa, Vincente Fox from Latin America, Corazon Aquino from Asia, John Kennedy from North America, and Charles DeGaulle from West Europe.)
4. The authoritarian aspects of India are tolerable because they are lessening, such as central control over the appointment of governors and the suspension of state parliaments.
   (No democracy allows for the suspension of provincial legislatures. Even China now elects provincial governors.)
5. The religious hatred aspects of India are tolerable because they are lessening. The Hindu Nationalist BJP Party leader has said that Moslems are welcome to join the party.
   (That is a little like the Ku Klux Klan saying it will accept Jews and African Americans as members if they accept the Klan's racist principles.)
6. Our people cannot speak English, and thus are not so capable of learning about the world's technology.
   (The reason they cannot speak English, though, is closely related to public policy which does not require English at the elementary and high school levels. Even China requires English, even though it associated with the United States and capitalism, or maybe because it is associated with the United States and capitalism. One can get directions to a hotel from a Chinese teenager more easily than from an Indian teenager, even though India was a former British colony, or maybe partly because of the resentment of being a former British colony.)

III. Win-Win Solutions to the Can't-Do Pairs

Under each of the eighteen pairs, there are two conflicting can't-do excuses. It is difficult to call one a conservative excuse and the other a liberal excuse, although that is often the case. It is, for example, the case that under wealth, conservatives are more likely to complain about lack of wealth and conservatives are more likely to complain about the evil influence of the rich. Under risk taking, however, the fear of unforeseen costs is could be either conservative or liberal depending on what the costs are. The important point is not classifying these conflicting excuses as conservative or liberal excuses, but rather developing policies that can satisfy both viewpoints.

A. Economic

Wealth. Likewise, all societies have a lack of per capita income. There is no normative ceiling on how high average incomes should be. Economic growth policies and job facilitators can increase national income and per capita income. People with money may have a tendency to use their money to buy favoritism in the political system or in other undesirable ways. Political favoritism can be effectively dealt with through public funding of elections so that candidates do not become dependent on rich campaign contributors in order to run for office.

Risk Taking. There is no question that taking risks can lead to some big monetary expenses and other costs. There is likewise no question that not taking risks can lead to some big missed opportunities. Win-win thinking tries to find ways through public policy whereby big risks can be taken so as to not miss important opportunities, but at the same time not suffer devastating costs. An example would be the government serving as an insurer for all new inventions for the first three years to give new inventors the opportunity to take out the bugs, but especially to give new inventors a willingness to put their products on the market. The insurance would only apply for three years or less, and only if the inventor submits material to indicate reasonable care has been exercised. This is how Jimmy Carter handles the swine flu vaccine.

Inequality Gap. It is far better to live in a society where the relatively poor have high average incomes, longevity, and educations, even though there is a big inequality gap, as contrasted to a society where the relatively poor have low average incomes, longevity, and educations, but so do the relatively rich. The gap can get too big and cause more antagonism than inspiration, but the low bottom is generally a much worse problem than the high gap.

Class Differences. Any kind of caste or class system which does not allow for upward mobility is likely to be a drag on merit treatment and national development. Class differences are desirable that inspire working class people to save for college educations for their children.

Corporations. Business can be evil, but so can government. The object is to structure the national and world economy to encourage doing good rather than evil. Competition stimulated by public policy is important, such as requiring utilities to rent their infrastructures at high rents to retailers of electricity, communications, and transportation. Also, vouchers that cannot be cashed in unless reasonable requirements are met, such as offering training where trainees pass tests and receive jobs for a minimum time period. Freed trade is global competition.

B. Technology

Technology. As already mentioned, it is possible to stimulate new technologies through tax incentives. It is simultaneously possible to not have such disruptive technology downsizing if the kind of job facilitators mentioned above are adopted to help displaced workers and executives to find new and better jobs.

World Resources. There seem to be no resources in the world that are not replaceable through modern science as contrasted to replaceable through zoology, botany, or geology. Modern science is capable of developing polymers to replace what was formerly covered by mining and metallurgy, including polymers for making automobiles that are lighter than aluminum and stronger than steel. Modern science as mentioned in discussing India can create new fusion and solar energy that is both more clean and more efficient than traditional oil and coal.

Food. There is obviously too much starvation and malnutrition in the world. There may also be too much pollution from insecticides, herbicides, and artificial fertilizer. Genetically modified plants can fight insects, weeds, and the lack of nutritious soil without the need for polluting chemicals. Genetic modification may thus be a great win-win for environmentalists and food producers, but there is a need to assure can't-do people that healthy genetic modification is a can-do possibility.

C. Social

Education. All societies have a lack of education in the sense that they can all benefit from people being better trained and thereby more productive, especially better trained to make use of new technologies. Having a better-trained population does not necessarily mean having more difficult-to-place Ph.D.'s as India supposedly does. So called over-educated people refer to people who have training for jobs that are already well-covered. They should be called mis-educated people rather than over-educated people. Such people can, however, be placed in productive jobs through the kind of job facilitators mentioned with regard to technology downsizing, including training vouchers, moving allowances, wage subsidies, placement commissions, and economic growth policies.

What Has Been Already Done. Likewise, countries should learn from their past history in avoiding mistakes and in adopting successful policies. Merely having already done something should mean little if the problem is still very much there. For example, a plaintiff should get no credit if the negotiator gets the defendant to go from $0 to $100 if the plaintiff has suffered damages of $500 and especially if the defendant might be willing to go as high as $600 in a win-win situation where the defendant gains greatly on some other track in multi-track or multi-criteria decision making.

Progress Being Made. In general, the U.S. and the world are doing very well in comparison to the past. They are, however, doing very poorly in comparison to what could be, but only if public policy works hard at it, not automatically by way of Adam Smith's invisible hand or Karl Marx's dialectical materialism.

Speaking English. This is a problem that came up in the Philippines where the choices for elementary school teaching were English, Taglog, or Filipino, versus a local dialect. Both the right-wing business people and the left-wing intellectual Communists recognized English as the win-win language. The business people recognized it as the language of commerce. The Communists recognized it as the language of science. Both recognized English as the language that would enable the Philippines to join the world in terms of business and science. This would be English, though, generally as a second language because the elementary students would have already learned Tagalog or the local dialect.

Religions Influence. Religion can play an inspirational role in development where people can consider it a religious obligation to try to improve the quality of life of humankind. That is the Golden Rule writ large. All major religions pay at least lip service to the Golden Rule. What is needed is more conversion of lip service into such actions as putting more food into starving mouths, especially of children. But not so much through charity as through teaching how to fish or better yet teaching how to make policy decisions on whether to encourage fishing, manufacturing, or other occupational activities in the world division of labor.

Population Size. A large population does provide more opportunities for geniuses, but it is much harder to feed, shelter, and clothe. The win-win approach is not to decrease the population, but instead to try to increase gross national product. One can then more adequately feed, shelter, and clothe the population. Also, try to encourage the middle class values of sending children to college, as they cause an almost automatic leveling in population.

D. Political

Party Systems. One can have diversity and meaningfulness simultaneously in a two-party system by allowing dissident groups within each party to assert themselves through direct primaries, ease of getting names on the ballot, and new forms of proportional representation within a two-party system, such as multi-member districts with cumulative voting.

Regionalism. Geographical divisions can be divisive if they are based on conquest as in the Russian Caucasus, but not if they are based on voluntary integration as in the European Union. International economic communities combine unity and autonomy in a win-win way.

E. International

Comparisons with Other Places. It is good to learn from other places. That means learning from places that have made mistakes to avoid and learning from places that have adopted successful policies. It is good to have role models and even to be envious, but not so good to be destructively jealous or to develop a sour grapes attitude.

F. Legal

Corruption. It is undesirable to have people receive jobs or contracts through bribes rather than through merit. It is, however, also undesirable to set up a surveillance system which destroys a willingness to take discretion and be creative. The criterion for success should be in the consequences. Thus, a system with some corruption that achieves high incomes, longevity, and education is better than one that is corruption free and low on those criteria. My father used to say that one cannot have a successful retail store without allowing the best help to occasionally steal.

All 18 of these items on the can't-do list are what might be called "Catch 22" excuses. That means terrible things happen if a country goes in one direction, and terrible things happen if a country goes in the opposite direction. Win-win analysis does not say "go West, left, or right, young man," but instead goes upward toward a super synthesis that can increase the benefits and decrease the costs without inherent tradeoffs, balancing, and can't-do excuses.

SECTION B: PEACE, PROSPERITY, AND DEMOCRACY

Chapter 14

RECIPROCAL RELATIONS AMONG PEACE, PROSPERITY, AND DEMOCRACY

The leading controversial policy issues in developing nations like those of South Asia tend to be economic, political, and military issues. The economic issues relate to how to make domestic economies more prosperous and how to facilitate investments, exports, and imports. The political issues relate to promoting democratic institutions, human rights, and self-determination. The military issues relate to non-proliferation of arms and reduction in regional conflicts.

The purpose of this article is to discuss some aspects of U.S. foreign policy as applied to these policy problems of developing regions and nations. The context is in terms of win-win thinking where all nations involved are better off as a result of the interaction. The context is also in terms of three tables which give a useful visual aids to clarify the mutually beneficial interaction.

I. TEN CAUSAL RELATIONS

The first six causal relations in Table 14-1 can be interpreted as follows:

1. Reduction in military conflicts is conducive to prosperity and investment.
2. Prosperity is conducive to reduction in military conflicts, especially prosperity based on buying and selling across countries that might otherwise be in conflict.
3. Prosperity is conducive to democratic institutions, human rights, and tolerance of minority ethnic groups.
4. Democracy, human rights, and ethnic peace are conducive to prosperity.
5. Democratic political institutions are also conducive to a reduction in military conflicts.
6. Reducing military conflicts is also conducive to democratic political institutions. The last four causal relations can be interpreted as follows:
7. U.S. policy is concerned with encouraging prosperity, investment, exporting, and importing because doing so is mutually beneficial.

8. U.S. policy is concerned with reducing military conflicts partly because of the favorable effect on prosperity and the economic issues.
9. U.S. policy is concerned with promoting a democratic political environment partly because of the favorable effect on prosperity and the economic issues.
10. U.S. domestic economic policy emphasizes U.S. prosperity and GNP growth which partly explains why U.S. international policy emphasizes mutually beneficial trade and investment opportunities.

Miscellaneous points include:

1. In the context of South Asia, Pakistan is especially concerned with military security; India is especially concerned with political issues; Sri Lanka is especially concerned with international economics; but all three countries are concerned with all three sets of issues.
2. The concept of mutual benefit is promoted through regional organizations, such as the south Asia Association for Regional Cooperation as well as through interregional interaction between South Asia and the U.S.
3. Social issues are also important such as poverty and ethnic groups, although they were considered under economic and political issues, respectively. Technology issues are also quite important, but they were discussed in the context of military, economic, and political issues.
4. There are positive relations among all five variables shown in Table 14-1. Those relations are positive in the sense of upward causation and being desirable relations, especially regarding promotion of peace, prosperity and democracy.

Table 14-1. Win-Win U.S. Foreign Policy

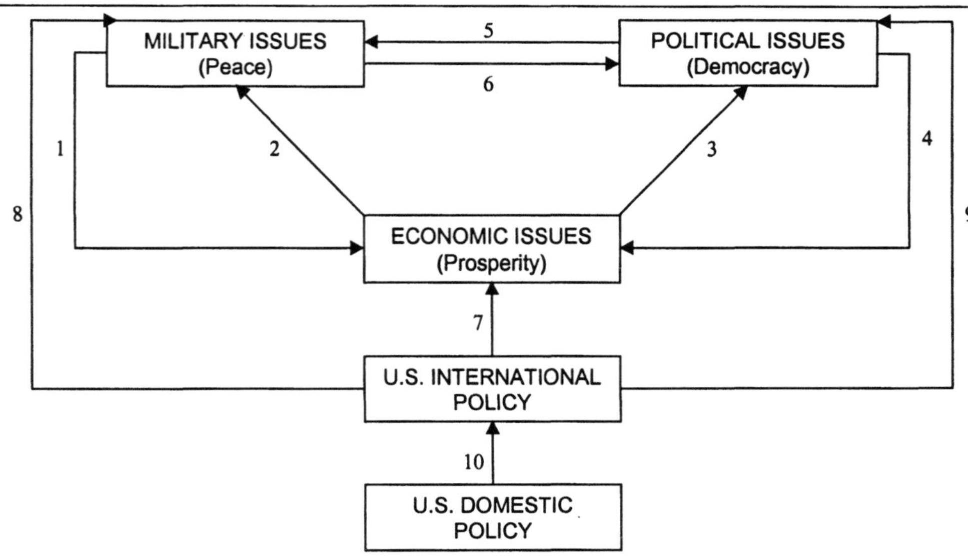

NOTE: All relations are positive. Thus there is no need for a plus sign on each arrow. For example, Relation 2 says prosperity causes peace because in time of depression, political leaders sometimes look for external enemies to distract people from being unemployed.

Table 14-2. U.S. Foreign Policy for 200 Years

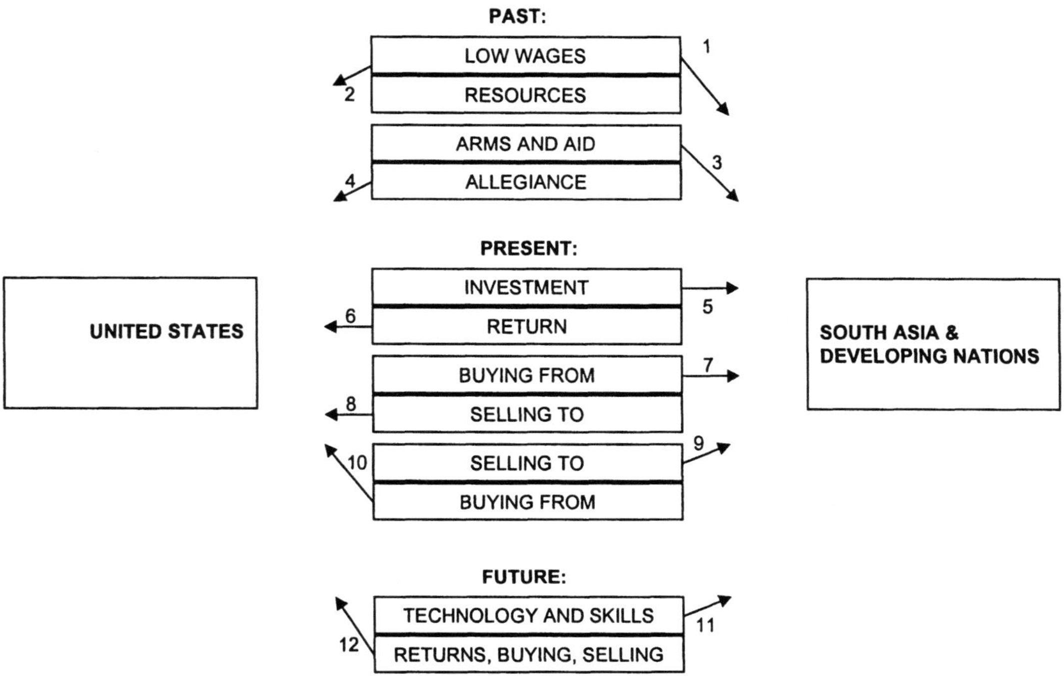

NOTE: Unlike Table 1, the arrows here are not causal arrows. The arrows on the left side show what the U.S. has generally received from its relations with developing nations in the past, present, and future. The arrows on the right side show what developing nations have received from the U.S.

II. HISTORICAL DEVELOPMENT

The past was characterized by colonialism and the Cold War. The present is being characterized by investment, importing, and exporting of funds and foods. The future may be characterized by transfer of technologies and skills from the U.S. which results in mutually beneficial investment-returns, buying, and selling. Those basic ideas are summarized in Table 14-2.

The arrows from the *past* indicate:

1 & 2. Colonialism involved low wages going to the developing nations, and valuable resources going to the United States or other industrialized nations.

3 & 4. The Cold War involved arms and aid going to developing nations and allegiance going to the U.S. or the Soviet Union.

The arrows from the *present* indicate:

5 & 6. Capital investment going to the developing nations with a reasonable return going back to the United States.

7 & 8. Cash or credits going to developing nations in return for their products.

9 & 10. Products going to developing nations in return for their cash or credits.

The arrows from the *future* indicate:

11 & 12. Technologies and skill go to developing nations thereby improving their ability to be good places for investment, buying, and selling.

In the past, there was often an imbalance with disproportionate benefits to the industrial nations and disproportionate detriments to the developing nations. In the present, there is generally mutual benefits from investments, exporting, and importing. In the future, the transfer of technologies and skills may enable all participating countries to exceed their best initial expectations simultaneously.

III. Illustrative Examples

Table 14-3, 14-4, and 14-5 show how win-win analysis might be applied to three key issues in South Asia. The issues relate to trade versus aid, secession, and nuclear arms.

A. Trade Versus Aid (Prosperity)

The U.S. currently tends to favor trade over aid, since trade is more mutually beneficial than aid which tends to mainly benefit the recipient nation unless there is a Cold War return.

Developing nations tend to favor aid with no strings attached, at least in the past, since they are fearful that (1) buying from the United States will disrupt local industries, and that (2) they have little to sell the United States.

Skills and technology transfer greatly benefit the United States by virtue of improving places for (1) U.S. investment, (2) the buying of American products, and (3) selling to the U.S. products needed by the American people. Skills and technology transfer benefit developing nations by enabling them to upgrade their international competitiveness even more than offering them either trade or aid.

B. Seceding (Democracy)

The U.S. tends to favor self-determination out of a regard for democratic decision-making and emphasizing the majority will within the rebellious provinces.

Developing nations tend to favor retaining their own rebellious provinces, emphasizing the majority will within the larger political entity.

Autonomy like a U.S. state refers to states having their own constitutions and governors that cannot be removed by Washington. States in India do not have their own constitutions and their governors can be removed by New Delhi.

Table 14-3. Trade Versus Aid in South Asia

Goals Alternatives	C Pro-U.S.	L Pro-South Asia
C Mainly Trade	+	-
L Self-determination	-	+
N 1. Some trade 2. Some aid	0	0
SOS OR WIN-WIN 1. Skills transfer 2. Technology transfer	++	++

Table 14-4. Secession in South Asia (Kashmir)

Goals Alternatives	C Pro-U.S.	L Pro-South Asia
C Self-determination	+	-
L 1. Retain rebellious provinces (Pro-India) 2. Release rebellious provinces (Pro-Pakistan)	-	+
N Partition	0	0
SOS OR WIN-WIN 1. Autonomy like a U.S. State	++	++

C. Nuclear Arms (Peace)

The U.S. tends to favor removal of nuclear arms from South Asia for fear that their presence may lead to nuclear warfare which might involve the United States directly or indirectly by way of the international disruption.

Countries which have nuclear capability like India and Pakistan are reluctant to weaken their deterrent power against each other.

Peaceful conversion in this context means providing India and Pakistan with the skills and technologies for converting their nuclear capability into peaceful and safe nuclear energy along with American investment funding.

Table 14-5. Nuclear Arms in South Asia

Goals Alternatives	C Pro-U.S.	L Pro-South Asia
C No nuclear arms	+	-
L Retain the capability that exists	-	+
N 1. Reduce 2. Inspect	0	0
SOS OR WIN-WIN Peaceful conversion	++	++

Chapter 15

PROSPECTS FOR GLOBAL PEACE, PROSPERITY, AND DEMOCRACY

I. PROSPECTS FOR DEMOCRACY

The prospects are good for democracy because:

1. Middle-class educated people are less likely to submit to an authoritarian government.
2. People who otherwise would have been dictators are now being socialized into being supportive of democracy.
3. The media make it difficult for dictators to lie to people. People can find out the truth through radio, TV, fax machines, phones, the internet, newspapers and books.
4. It is difficult to rely on an army of volunteers as contrasted to mercenaries or professional soldiers. Mercenaries and volunteers who do so due to lack of employment opportunities are not so prevalent when jobs are readily available. Also, the people in the military have been socialized into democratic values as a result of education systems.
5. There are lots of precedents for how to bring down dictators such as massing the public as was done in Yugoslavia and the Philippines, or having a person succeed to the office of dictator who has been socialized in modern democracy such as Gorbachev. Also labor unions are more educated and sophisticated with regard to winning friends and influencing people, as indicated by the Solidarity movement in Poland and the relative inability of unions to get very far in the 1800s throughout the world and in the 1900s in the United States.
6. The influence of the U.S. is favorable toward democracy now that the Cold War is over.
7. Also countries want to promote democracy on the part of other countries because democracy leads to greater productivity and prosperity, and it makes other countries into better customers, suppliers, investment outlets, sources of investment money.
8. The establishment of multi-lateral international economic communities is a good influence, like the European union.

9. The ending of the Cold War is important in many countries for promoting democracy. During the Cold War there were constant battles between the extreme left and the extreme right, both of whom were authoritarian. The extreme right justified its authoritarianism on the grounds of a threat from the extreme left and vice versa. The U.S. is no longer aiding the extreme right, and the Soviet Union is no longer aiding the extreme left.

II. Prospects for Prosperity

The reasons for future prosperity looking good are:

1. We have gotten away from the idea that the way to fight inflation or too many dollars chasing too few goods is to decrease the number of dollars by raising interest rates. That has the effect of causing a recession or even a depression because raising interest rates means that virtually all businesses have to cut back. They nearly all borrow money for raw materials, merchandise for resale, expansion, and other activities in anticipation that the profit rate will be higher than the interest rate unless the interest rate goes up.
2. We are now fighting inflation or too many dollars chasing too few goods by increasing the quantity of goods through methods to increase productivity such as improving training, new technologies, free trade, and competition.
3. New technologies are increasing productivity. By doing so, each worker is able to produce more and earn more and spend more. The increased spending makes for jobs for displaced workers and firms, although they may need retraining and other job facilitators. We are undergoing a computer-internet revolution which is generating lots of new technologies and new ways of being more productive and will do so for some time to come.
4. New technologies tend to lead to other new technologies in a geometrical progression or an exponential curve. On a rough average, each invention or knowledge discovery leads to two or more other inventions. A given subfield may plateau out after awhile such as automobiles. But the transportation technology grows with the development of airplanes. Old subfields that have plateaued out frequently get revived, such as the revival of auto transportation by hybrid cars and other cars that do not rely so heavily on internal combustion and fossil fuels.
5. New training is rapidly occurring as people acquire more recognition than ever of the importance of education and training, for themselves and their children. New training also has a multiplier effect in the sense that by learning how to read, one can then learn how to be a better automobile mechanic. Likewise, by learning how to read an automotive repair manual, one can be inspired to become a mechanical engineer. Thus, training builds on training just as technology builds on technology. We are now in a time period when new training technologies are being rapidly developed, such as computer learning, internet learning, learning by way of CDs, tapes, TV, radio, and other devices to supplement the traditional professor at one end of a log or one end of a classroom.

6. Prosperity builds on competitive free enterprise, especially with regard to such essential services for business and the economy as electricity and communications. We are now moving into requiring the renting of infrastructures so as to facilitate competitive electricity and variations on telephoning. This is to the benefit of businesses, consumer clubs, and even the original monopolies who now make more money by renting their infrastructures. That kind of competition leads to consumers and businesses may be demanding other forms of competition, such as allowing foreign airlines to carry passengers from one American city to another and in allowing foreign electrical companies and telephone companies to sell in the U.S. by renting existing infrastructures which mainly consist of electric lines and telephone lines.
7. Free trade is expanding and generating long-term prosperity. That includes free trade in products but also free trade in ideas and in people. The movement of ambitious people to places where opportunities are greater is probably the key reason for U.S. prosperity. Ambitious immigrants keep feeding our labor supply, and their children and grandchildren become our future professors, lawyers, doctors, and government officials. Free trade in people also encourages countries to become more attractive to tourists, foreign students, skilled workers, immigrants, and others to the benefit of those who are already here as well as those who are encouraged to come.
8. Public policy is improving its effectiveness and efficiency with regard to promoting prosperity. This involves such innovative ideas or variations on them such as the use of vouchers, contracting out, and performance payment. Vouchers can get businesses and people to spend money to increase their productivity by putting up matching amounts or supplements. Contracting out can specify the provisions for a quality workplace, consumer protection, environmental protection, and a competitive marketplace more so than old fashioned capitalism or socialism. Performance payment obviously produces better performance than any kind of hourly payment, flat fees, or relatively fixed salaries. Performance payment can be much more widely applied in the private sector and the public sector, including education, police, health care, finding jobs for displaced workers, developing new technologies, and other desired activities.
9. The future looks good for prosperity partly because the world is at peace. The cold war is over. Countries are making too much money selling and buying from each other to go to war with each other. War is destructive of the development of education, civilian technologies, and world competition, as well as people and property. There is no sign of a world war in the future or even wars among sovereign states. Most of the internal wars are leftovers from the cold war. This is true of the four wars in Angola and the Congo.
10. The future looks good for prosperity because democracy is on the increase. Democracy leads to more effective, efficient, and equitable economies by virtue of the free circulation of ideas. Democracies are less likely to start wars than dictatorships. Dictators have a tendency to start wars to distract people from inefficiencies in the economy. Under a dictatorship, it is hard for the people to protest going to war.
11. All those points add up to saying that the prospects for prosperity look good. That, however, is not because of the invisible hand of Adam Smith or the dialectic

materialism of Karl Marx. It is largely because of conscious training for using them, competitive marketplaces, and free trade. Prosperity will not continue and expand automatically. It does not occur by the will of God who gives human beings free will to wreck their economies. Economies flourish well when that free will is wisely exercised by adopting public policies that promote prosperity or in a broader sense that promote prosperity, peace, and democracy.

III. PROSPECTS FOR PEACE

We need to talk about the prospects for peace. There is less to say on that subject but we could mention the following:

1. Democracy makes for peace, as was discussed under point 9 of the prosperity section above. Since democracy is increasing, peace is also increasing.
2. Prosperity also makes for peace, as was discussed under point 10 of the prosperity section above. Since prosperity is increasing, peace is also increasing.
3. Peace is increasing in itself regardless of prosperity and democracy, largely because the Cold War is over. That confrontational interaction between the U.S. and the Soviet Union almost destroyed the world in what could have been a nuclear holocaust. The Cold War ended largely because the people and the leadership in the Soviet Union could not continue to accept a dictatorship of the proletariat more than 70 years after the Revolution. No longer could the government justify a dictatorship on the grounds that there were forces seeking to restore the Russian monarchy or there were capitalist forces. The rest of the world was dominated by political parties that had largely accepted the 10 points of the Communist Manifesto of 1848.
4. The Soviet Union had, in effect, planted the seeds or had developed the internal inconsistencies that inevitably led to democratizing the dictatorship. From the start in 1917, Lenin made it clear that the Soviet Union would have to quickly educate its population, if it was going to amount to anything. The need for an educated population was accepted by all subsequent Soviet leaders, including Stalin, Khrushchev, and Gorbachev. The educated population eventually decided that they were no longer illiterate or semi-literate peasants or factory workers. They were now mainly educated, white collar workers and farmers and factory workers who were also well educated for working with modern technologies. That kind of educated population cannot be dictated to, and Gorbachev did not seem to want to be a dictator. He was the first Soviet prime minister who was not a professional Bolshevik or politician but who had been trained with graduate training to be an engineer. He was never a revolutionary on the barricades. He was born many years after the revolution. Unlike most of his predecessors, especially Lenin, Stalin, and Khrushchev.
5. Republicans like to say that Reagan won the Cold War by bankrupting the Soviet Union. That seems a bit questionable in light of the above facts. More important, given the definition of bankruptcy, Reagan came closer to bankrupting the United States than the Soviet Union. He incurred more national debt through his Cold War

arms program than all the previous presidents put together. The $2 trillion national debt became almost $5 trillion by the time he left office. If things had not drastically changed shortly thereafter, the pressure on interest rates might have caused a depression, as a result of the government constantly having to borrow to pay off the treasury bonds that constantly came due. Fortunately, from 1992 to the year 2000, the gross national product more than doubled, from $4 trillion to over $8 trillion. That was enough to wipe out the annual deficit and set things in the direction of enabling the national debt to be virtually wiped out by approximately 2010. In other words, the wild spending of the Reagan years probably did not end the Cold War, but the end of the Cold War played a big part in the present and future prosperity of the U.S.

6. Much to Reagan's credit in ending the Cold War is his personal involvement, not his $300 billion military budgets and huge deficit spending. He did meet with Gorbachev in Iceland in about 1985, which began the move toward the end of the Cold War. It probably officially ended on December 21, 1991, when the Soviet Union dissolved into 16 separate countries. Only Reagan could have made peace with the Soviet Union the way he did. Lyndon Johnson and other democrats would have been afraid of being accused of being soft on communism. In view of how Lyndon Johnson handled the Vietnam War, he might have found some way to go to war with Khrushchev rather than to go to the peace table.
7. There is nothing currently in existence in the world that is likely to lead to the kind of bipolar war-generating environment that existed from 1945 to 1990 between the capitalistic U.S. and the communist USSR, between the fascist axis and the relatively democratic allies between 1920 and 1945, or between the Anglo-French imperialists and the German imperialists from about 1870 to 1920. Before that, it was largely the Napoleonic French revolutionaries versus the British monarchy from about 1780 to 1870. Before that, wars were rather local rather than world wars or even wars that covered Europe and North America. We have not reached the end of ideology, in the sense that there are no conservative or liberal viewpoints but only neutral viewpoints. We do seem to have reached a point in much of the world where conservatives and liberals, like George W. Bush and Al Gore, may represent real differences and get highly emotional, but there is no significant authoritarian right or authoritarian left, if significant means getting more than five or ten percent of the vote.
8. Sometimes people looking for a new cold war will try to find that China is the new evil empire. It certainly has a big population, and nuclear capability, and a big army. It is, however, an impoverished country with per capita income of less than $1,000 per person. It is undergoing rapid economic growth, but that makes the country more oriented toward international trade than international war. Of special importance, we should note that China is moving in a democratic direction, even if it is presently a one-party dictatorship. One measure is that governors and mayors are now chosen by contested elections in the provinces and cities. They were always chosen by Beijing or Peking, going back to the time of Confucius or before. The internet has become a lively source of constructive and not so constructive criticism of the government, which the government tolerates out of recognition of the economic benefits of the internet.

The Chinese dictatorship may be largely a generational phenomenon. Their revolution was 1949, not 1917. Their leadership is still filled with people from the Great March. Their children, however, led the anti-party revolution of Tiananmen Square in 1989. People's University, which is the university especially for children of party officials, was much more active in the guerilla warfare of Tiananmen Square than the poetry-reading and poetry-writing students of Peking University. The People's University students of 1989, who will be the next generation of leaders, especially objected to such corruption indicators as officials from the Ministry of Automotives and Electronics driving around in Japanese cars with chauffeurs who stand in front of the car all day in order to make the officials look important. The students also considered it an outrage that orange-pop salesmen in front of the gates of the university made more money than political science professors. With attitudes like that, these future leaders should be more sensitive to principles of democracy.

Chapter 16

INTERNATIONAL PEACE, PROSPERITY, AND DEMOCRACY

Win-win international studies involves applying win-win analysis to problems of international peace, prosperity, and democracy. Win-win analysis refers to analyzing a policy problem in such a way as to determine what alternative might be proposed that would enable conservatives, liberals, and other major viewpoints to all come out ahead of their best initial expectations simultaneously.

In this article, win-win analysis is applied to peace issues that relate to U.S. foreign policy since the Cold War and to relations between the United States and the United Nations. The analysis is applied to prosperity issues that relate to tariffs and exchange rates. The analysis is also applied to democracy issues that relate to promoting international democracy through trade and other means.

All of these applications view peace, prosperity, and democracy in an international or multi-national context rather than in a domestic context, as was done in a related article in the spring 2001 issue of "Peace, Prosperity, and Democracy." There the peace problem was the problem of domestic violence due to drug addicts seeking money to pay for drugs or seeking territory for the sale of drugs. The prosperity problem was dealing with inflation and unemployment simultaneously. The democracy problem was facilitating voter turnout.

I. WIN-WIN PEACE ANALYSIS

A. U.S. Foreign Policy Since Cold War

Cold War U.S. foreign policy divided conservatives and liberals. Conservatives tended to favor right-wing governments and large defense expenditures, whereas liberals tended to favor left-wing governments and lower defense expenditures. Now, both sides support lower defense expenditures and are less influenced by the economic ideology of foreign governments.

The prevailing conservative orientation seems more isolationist and less interventionist than the current liberal orientation. That is shown in the greater liberal support for intervention in Bosnia, Somalia, and other places where peacemaking or humanitarian aid might be appropriate. A compromise position would advocate greater selectivity in the application of isolationism or peacemaking.

Table 1. U.S. Foreign Policy Since the Cold War

Goals / Alternatives	CONS Save taxes and promote business	LIB Peace and promote employment
CONS Isolationism	+	-
LIB Peace-making	-	+
NEUTRAL Selective peace-making	0	0
SOS OR WIN-WIN Peace as part of larger international package	++	++

Table 2. U.S. and the U.N.

Goals / Alternatives	CONS Save U.S. dollars and lives	LIB World peace
CONS Minimum U.S. involvement (Isolationism)	+	-
LIB Substantial U.S. involvement (Intervention)	-	+
NEUTRAL Some of each	0	0
SOS OR WIN-WIN Volunteer U.N. force	++	++

The key conservative goal seems to be to save taxes and promote domestic business. The key liberal goal seems to be to promote peace in the workplace and domestic employment opportunities.

An SOS solution might be to see peace as part of a larger international package. That foreign-policy package would include the United States actively promoting peace, prosperity, and democracy throughout the world in order to help all nations become better customers for the United States, suppliers to the United States, places for investment, and better world citizens. That kind of pragmatic policy would be mutually beneficial in increasing the national incomes and quality of life in both the United States and elsewhere.

Separate analyses could be developed. An important factor in promoting peace is supporting the United Nations' peacemaking activities. An important factor in promoting prosperity is free trade in the movement of products, factories, and labor. An important factor in promoting democracy is the free movement of ideas through the mass media and providing financial and technical support for democratic forces inside and outside potentially dictatorial governments.

B. The U.S. and the U.N.

The key conservative goal in this context, relating to the role of the US in helping the UN to bring peace to Bosnia, is to save US dollars and save lives. The conservatives weren't always so oriented toward isolation. They were very interventionist back In the days of the cold war, especially with regards to curtailing the expansion of the Soviet Union. But at the present time, they do espouse more of an isolationist, less of an intervention policy than liberals do. The conservative alternative for saving US dollars and lives is to keep US troops at home. They feel it's more important to develop the US first. The liberals, on the other hand, are more oriented toward being the policemen of the world traveling around with the goal of promoting world peace. More idealistic or maybe more naive, they believe what is sometimes referred to as a social worker ideology. That necessitates intervention.

The win-win solution saves US dollars, US lives, and promotes world peace simultaneously. An approach recommended by some who specialize in international relations is the idea of a volunteer UN force. What this would mean is that American troops would not be sent to Bosnia, Somalia, or anywhere else. The UN would have its own volunteer force, a force similar to the French Foreign Legion. It would consist of people from all over the world who would join partly out of idealism, partly because it pays some money. They would not be allowed to join unless they've had some military experience or some aptitude for military training. It would provide an opportunity for Vietnam War veterans, Russian soldiers who had fought in Afghanistan, and others to participate in a force which would be devoted to a righteous cause. The officers would be officers who had served in the militaries of their various countries.

As a result there would be no American soldiers in this UN force. There may be Americans in the UN force, but they would be Americans acting on their own. They would be volunteering to serve. They would not be drafted, or as in the case of the current Americans serving in Bosnia, ordered to go because their unit was called. They are not completely volunteers. These would be pure volunteers, pure in the sense they would be joining the UN force with the agreement to go wherever they are sent. If they won't go, for ideological or other reasons, then an option can be provided where they can quit. In such a case it might be fair to have them pay back something in return for their training. Such an arrangement has many possibilities.

Such a plan has been opposed in the past by the US because it was feared that the UN could not be trusted to have its own volunteer force. Strictly by the numbers, the UN in the past has been too much under the control of developing nations or nations under the control of the Soviet Union. But now, with the breakup of the Soviet Union, the US dominates the UN as the only super power in the world. The volunteer force could not be a threat to the US. Though a bit behind in its payments, the US is the leading source of funds to the UN, which further adds to its influence. If the US doesn't like what the volunteer force is doing, it could just cut off the funding, use its veto power in the Security Council, or use its influence among countries of the world. This kind of volunteer force would mean that no American lives or American dollars would be used, yet it could still be very effective in promoting world peace. It's possible that the volunteer force might call upon member countries to supply additional troops at some time, but this would be handled as the need arose. This represents another kind of win-win solution.

The feasibility problem for this issue is psychological. It would be conceived that such a force might represent the muscle behind some type of world government which could partly deprive the US or its sovereignty. Some might fear the volunteer force is going to march in and take over. As with all the other obstacles, it's necessary for this one to be overcome if this win-win solution is going to be adopted. People have to realize that a UN volunteer might not be a threat to them. In no way would the people with blue helmets serving in Bosnia invade the US.

II. International Prosperity Analysis

A. Tariffs

U.S. exporters and investors are helped by free trade with Mexico and other places because (1) Mexicans can buy more U.S. products if there are no Mexican tariffs artificially raising the price of American products, (2) Mexicans can buy more U.S. products if they have more income as a result of working in factories that have expanded as a result of American capital, and (3) U.S. investors can make money and add to the U.S. GNP by investing in Mexican factories which are now able to export better to the U.S. because U.S. tariffs have been dropped.

U.S. consumers are helped by free trade with Mexico and other places because (1) they can buy products made in Mexico at lower prices because they no longer have a U.S. tariff artificially raising the prices, (2) they can benefit from low prices that should result from decreased labor expenses associated with some products made in Mexico, possibly stimulated with American capital, and (3) U.S. consumers include business firms that buy producer goods less expensively from Mexico and thereby make American firms more internationally competitive.

U.S. firms and workers who are not sufficiently competitive would be hurt by the NAFTA agreement, but this can be minimized by (1) retraining workers and firms so they can be more competitive in their old products or new products, (2) side agreements with Mexico that require upgrading of labor standards in Mexico, and (3) disrupted workers and firms may benefit from the increased prosperity of the U.S. as a result of more exporting, better overseas investing, and better buys for U.S. consumers.

Mexicans can benefit in the same ways as Americans by just substituting for the three goal-columns (1) Mexican exporters and investors, (2) non-competitive Mexican firms and workers, and (3) Mexican consumers.

The opponents of NAFTA are referred to in this table as conservatives, and the advocates are referred to as liberals. That is done partly to simplify the calculation of the tools. It is also in accordance with the fact that conservatives have traditionally been in favor of high tariffs, although in recent years that is less true than from about 1800 through the 1930's.

Table 3. Tariffs

Goals / Alternatives	CONS 1. Non-competitive U.S. firms and workers	LIB 1. U.S. exporters and investors 2. U.S. consumers
CONS 1. Opponents. 2. Labor unions and weak business firms.	+	-
LIB 1. Advocates. 2. Intellectual liberals. 3. Business interests.	-	+
NEUTRAL 1. Middling.	0	0
SOS OR WIN-WIN 1. Free trade. 2. Retraining. 3. Side agreements. 4. Expanding the economy.	++	++

B. Exchange Rates

A high dollar value means that $1 will buy many units of the currencies of other countries. A low dollar value means that $1 will buy relatively few units of the currencies of other countries.

If the dollar has a relatively high value, then we have difficulty selling to other countries because they have to give a lot of units of their currencies in order to get a dollar. If the dollar has relatively low value, then we have difficulty buying from other countries because Americans have to give a lot of dollars in order to get the currencies of other countries.

If we concentrate on improving the quality and prices of American goods, then we can sell a lot of American goods to other countries without lowering the value of the dollar. A big effect of selling a lot more to other countries is the increase in the American national income. That enables us to have a lot more money to buy from other countries without raising the value of the dollar.

Thus improving the quality and price of American goods through upgrading technologies and skills is a good SOS solution because it can achieve both goals of increased buying and increased selling simultaneously. This is in contrast to manipulating the dollar which increases one goal but decreases the other goal in a typical tradeoff pattern. See Table 5-4.

The SOS alternative also recognizes that trade, even without human rights conditions, can promote human rights by promoting prosperity and internal education. Democratic institutions can also promote prosperity and trade. There is thus reciprocal causation, even without explicitly linking the two.

Trade when used to encourage human rights needs to be presented more as a reward or bribe, rather than as a threat or punishment. Trade has worked well to encourage democratic institutions in places like South Africa. It can backfire if trade is withdrawn to the point where extremists come to power (as in Russia), or to the point where the economy suffers long-term destruction (as could happen in Haiti).

Trade can also be used as a bargaining chip for other purposes besides human rights conditions, such as tariff reductions and the opening of investment opportunities, which conservatives would endorse also.

Table 4. Exchange Rates

Goals **Alternatives**	**CONS** **Buy from other countries**	**LIB** **Sell to other countries**
CONS High dollar value	+	-
LIB Low dollar value	-	+
NEUTRAL Middle dollar value	0	0
SOS OR WIN-WIN Improve quality and price of U.S. goods	++	++

III. Win-Win Democracy Analysis

This analysis stems largely from the controversy over how far to go in withholding trade from China until human rights are given more recognition. The problem, however, applies to many countries that would like increased trade with the United States, but lack a minimum level of domestic institutions.

The conservative position is to have trade without human rights conditions or prerequisites. The liberal position is to use trade to secure better human rights conditions, including the possibility of a pluralistic political system which allows two or more political parties to meaningfully compete for votes. A neutral position would think in terms of less substantial human rights such as visits by Red Cross workers to political prisoners, but not ending political prisoners.

The conservative position is oriented toward American business profits. The liberal position is oriented toward spreading democracy. Both sides endorse each other's goals, but not with equal weight.

The object of a SOS alternative would be to promote both trade and human rights, partly through education and communication. That means encouraging students from China and other such countries to come to the United States. Doing so means they are more likely to return with American values like democracy. That also means increasing the communication of democracy-related ideas by way of radio, television, newspapers, books, and other forms of communication to China and other such countries.

The SOS alternative also recognizes that trade, even without human rights conditions, can promote human rights by promoting prosperity and internal education. Democratic institutions can also promote prosperity and trade. There is thus reciprocal causation, even without explicitly linking the two.

Trade when used to encourage human rights needs to be presented more as a reward or bribe, rather than as a threat or punishment. Trade has worked well to encourage democratic institutions in places like South Africa. It can backfire it trade is withdrawn to the point where extremists come to power (as in Russia), or to the point where the economy suffers long-term destruction (as could happen in Haiti).

Trade can also be used as a bargaining chip for other purposes besides human rights conditions, such as tariff reductions and the opening of investment opportunities, which conservatives would endorse also.

Table 5. Promoting International Democracy

Goals **Alternatives**	**CONS** **Business profits**	**LIB** **Spread democracy**
CONS Trade without human rights conditions.	+	-
LIB Trade with human rights conditions.	-	+
NEUTRAL Trade with slight conditions.	0	0
SOS OR WIN-WIN Promoting trade and rights partly through education and communications.	++	++

PART THREE: PROCESS

SECTION A: CREATIVITY

Chapter 17

CREATIVE LEGISLATION IN THE U.S. IN THE 1900S

The purpose of this article is to pick a top dozen regarding federal legislation in the 1900s, then ask what they tend to have in common, which might explain these public policy innovations. By a dozen, we mean congressional legislation that most historians would consider reasonably momentous in American political history. Momentous refers to congressional debate, impact, and relevant literature.

I. THE TOP DOZEN CONGRESSIONAL STATUTES

A. Economic Policy

(1) Unemployment and inflation. Establishment of the Federal Reserve System.

(2) Consumer policy in creating anti-trust and FTC. In the economic field, the Sherman and Clayton Anti-Trust Act, Federal Trade Commission, and the Pure Food and Drug Act.

(3) Labor policy including NLRA. The Wagner Act or National Labor Relation Act, along with the Taft-Hartley amendments and fair labor standards.

B. Social Policy

(4) Poverty including social security in the 1930s, but key court decisions in the 1960s. That recognizes that policy can come from the President like Keynesian policy, and from the courts, like poverty policy. Social Security, which covers a lot of subprograms regarding children, the blind, the disabled, and the aged.

(5) Civil rights. The Civil Rights Statutes, especially 1964 on Fair Employment, also 1965 on Voting Rights, 1968 on Housing, and 1957 and 1963 on Education. We could divide merit treatment into two, the legislation referred to above is civil rights legislation that relates to ethnic and gender discrimination. We could have a category that deals with other kinds of discrimination. Then, we would talk about

the ADA which is the disability legislation. We would also talk about the anti-age discrimination. We could talk about hate crimes, but that is a state legislation.

C. Technology Policy

(6) Environment. The legislation of the early 1970s under Nixon regarding air and water, and solid waste under Reagan.

(7) Health policy, which includes Medicaid and Medicare. One could include the Clinton HMO program, but it did not pass. Before Medicaid and Medicare, we had money under the Hill-Burton Act money for hospitals provided that they serve the poor.

(8) Energy. The 1996 legislation that provides for deregulation of the sale of electricity and communications was a monumental piece of legislation. We could talk about the deregulation and competition-promoting legislation in general. That would include deregulation for the airlines and deregulation of interstate commerce. Some of that deregulation occurred under Reagan with regard to transportation. The deregulation with regard to electricity and communications had been under Clinton.

D. Political Policy

(9) Free speech and civil liberties. That is the Supreme Court, not Congress or the President. However, the Internet of 2001 is a great free speech facilitator. Congress deserves no credit for that, they tried to interrupt with censorship legislation.

(10) Motor voter registration.

E. International Policy

(11) World peace. The Marshall Plan, the Peace Corps, and AIDS programs. Much of what has come out of the federal government with regard to world peace from 1945 to about 1995 has been Cold War activities which have resulted in numerous wars throughout the world, not peace, including Vietnam, Korea, Central America, Central Africa, and Central Asia. It is disproportionately the central part of developing regions that are most impoverished and isolated, most subject to manipulation, and also where Americans have the least respect for human life. This is well illustrated with Guatemala, Nicaguara, and El Salvador in Latin America. It is well illustrated with the Congo, South Africa, Ethiopia, and Yuganda in Africa. And also so well illustrated with Mosambeek, Angloia, Rwanda, and Burawandi. These are the American killing fields, far worse than anything in Cambodia. For Asia, it is Cambodia, Laos, Vietnam, Afghanistan, Iraq, and Iran. Not much can honestly be said for American peace policy in the 20th century, or at least the second half of it. Government reform is partly a Supreme Court area with regard to the redistricting of state legislatures.

(12) International trade. NAFTA, GATT, China trade, and tariff reduction for Africa and poor countries. The Clinton Free Trade Statutes like NAFTA, GATT, and maybe the new legislation dropping tariffs involving imports from poor countries in Africa and elsewhere.

II. TYPES OF POLICY INNOVATION

Did these occur during a Democratic or Republican administration? I can predict that under the Democrats, the innovation probably favors the minorities. If under Republicans, the innovation probably favors business and well-to-do people.

Did the innovation occur during a time of war, depression, or prosperity? If during a time of war, I would predict that there would be no innovations. If in a time of depression, the innovations would be some anti-depressing activity. That does not give much predictability. We have only had one depression in the 20th century. We may never have another one. Prosperity is good for innovation, which actually runs contrary to some common sense. One would think that in bad times people would welcome change, but the opposite may be true. In bad times, people are filled with anxiety. They certainly cannot tolerate change very well if it means increased rights for women, minorities, or labor. Maybe they can tolerate change for consumers because everyone is a consumer.

Prosperity is also important because many of these programs cost money, and it helps to have more revenue coming in to the federal government than expense. That may not be true. Under traditional recession-fighting economies, the government is supposed to do its big spending when times are bad, in order to pump money into the economy. Most of these programs do not cost big money anyhow. There is no big money involved in prohibiting discrimination on the basis of race or gender.

These innovations can definitely be classified by substance, which will help think of what the innovations might be. Substance includes economic, technology, social, political, international, and legal.

III. CAUSES OF CREATIVE LEGISLATION

Possible explanations for why these legislative innovations occurred when they did might include the following:

1. Political parties
2. Personalities
3. Crisis situations
4. Social forces, movements, and interest groups
5. Political and social science

Partisan factors are observable. Nearly all the examples occurred during Democratic administrations. The Democrats are more in favor of change and innovation. Environmental protection is more of a middle class activity than the others. Likewise, deregulation tends to be a pro-business activity for businesses that want to enter into the market to buy products.

Not all Democrats as Presidents are equally innovative. The key Presidents were Wilson, Roosevelt, Kennedy, Johnson, and Clinton. There is nothing very innovative about the other Democratic Presidents, although there have not been very many others in the 20th century. The others include just two: Truman and Carter. We cannot do much generalizing from that small of a sample. We could say that presidents that serve two terms have more of an opportunity to do good legislation. The causal direction may be the opposite, meaning that doing good legislation gets them re-elected.

One can argue that crisis situations provoke the legislation and who happens to be President is irrelevant. That seems to be untrue if the biggest crisis we have had in the 20th century have been wars. World War I, World War II, the Korean War, the Vietnam War, and the Cold War stimulated no creativity. They stifled creativity. The depression may have stimulated some creativity with regard to labor legislation and social security, but that is only two of the ten.

One can think in terms of social forces as part of a kind of historical dialectic, going into the start of the 20th century or going back to the start of the 19th century. The landed aristocrats controlled the U.S. and Western Europe. The new merchant class rose up partly through factory technology and trading technology with regard to transportation. They overthrew the landed aristocrats in the French Revolution, and the American Revolution, but that does not mean legislation. It means the U.S. Constitution, the Bill of Rights, and the French Constitution. Nothing much happened, though, until the end of the 1900s, especially the beginning of the 20th century in the U.S. when labor rose up against factory managers and owners and established labor legislation in the 1930s. Before that, consumers rose up and established pro-consumer legislation under Woodrow Wilson. Then in the 1960s, minorities and women rose up and established civil rights legislation. In the 1970s, there was an environmental movement. In the 1980s, a deregulation movement. In the 1990s, a free trade movement. What all these movements have in common is the need for a large influential block of people to object to existing conditions and to push or demand for remedial legislation.

Since our audience is academics, disproportionately, we should say something about the role of academics:

1. Woodrow Wilson had a Ph.D. in political science and was a professor of public administration at Princeton. Then he was president of Princeton.
2. FDR had a brain trust that included especially Charles Merriam from the political science department at the University of Chicago, who is considered one of the founders of modern political science.
3. We then move up to the Kennedy-Johnson period. Especially Kennedy, but also Johnson. The leading description of the Kennedy administration is a book by Halberstam entitled *The Best and the Brightest*. It emphasizes all the academic types. As for political scientists, the closest name that stands out is Arthur Slusinger, a historian. One should note that FDR had lots of law professors like Felix Frankfurter before he was appointed to the Supreme Court.

IV. SOME REFERENCES

An interesting book on creative legislation is Nelson Polsby, *Political Innovation in America: The Politics of Policy Initiation* (Yale, 1984). This book deals with eight legislative case studies on which information could be readily obtained, rather than eight or a dozen examples of highly important or creative legislation. To some extent, the Polsby book illustrates social science research that focuses on less important units of analysis where the light is good, rather than on key units where information is not so readily available.

Polsby finds that the underlying causes of political innovation are having an innovation-prone culture and having needs. The U.S. may be an innovative culture on technology matters, but it has not been so innovative on public policy. Almost all 12 of the above examples of creative legislation were adopted in earlier years by countries in Western Europe. The U.S. may lag behind on egalitarian policies because immigration tends to push people up without requiring public policy to do so. Saying that the second most important factor is need is like the cliche that necessity is the mother of invention. What we are concerned with is not so much why public policies have been adopted, but why they get adopted when they do. Since the need may long precede the adoption, and the adoption stays after the need is past.

Other relevant books include the literature that deals with agenda setting and policy formulation. That literature does talk about what causes or triggers the process of creative legislation. The literature includes:

1. James Anderson (1997). *Public Policy Making: An Introduction*. Boston: Houghton Mifflin.
2. Christopher Basso (1994). "The Practice and Study of Policy Formation" in S. Nagel (ed.), *Encyclopedia of Policy Studies*. New York: Marcel Dekker.
3. Garry Brewer and Peter DeLeon (1983). *The Foundations of Policy Analysis*. Homewood: Dorsey Press.
4. Robert Eyestone (ed.) (1984). *Public Policy Formation*. Stamford: JAI Press.
5. Larry Gertson (1997). *Public Policy Making: Process and Principles*. Armonk: M.E. Sharpe.
6. Charles Jones (1984). *An Introduction to the Study of Public Policy*. Pacific Grove: Brooks/Cole.
7. John Kingdon (1984). *Agendas, Alternatives, and Public Policies* Boston: Little, Brown.

Chapter 18

EFFECTS OF PUBLIC POLICY ON STIMULATING CREATIVITY

Win-win analysis involves finding solutions to diverse problems, especially policy problems whereby all major sides can come out ahead of their best initial expectations. In policy problems, this tends to mean that both conservatives and liberals come out ahead of their best expectations.

In discussing the win-win aspects of creativity, we are concerned with such issues as (1) how to encourage creativity without consumers being taken advantage of, (2) how to encourage creativity without overly subsidizing relevant business firms, (3) how to develop the right combination of hands-off and government stimulation to encourage creativity, (4) how to develop research findings that are both valid and simple, and (5) how to strive for generalizations and case studies, simultaneously.

I. THE PATENT SYSTEM AND ENCOURAGING INVENTIONS

Preserving the patent system (as it is currently operating) tends to stifle some creativity by providing for a 17-year monopoly renewable once, but frequently renewed repeatedly with slight variations. It also stifles creativity by being the basis for lawsuits designed to obtain injunctions against creative competition. See Table 18-1.

Abolishing patents can hurt some creativity on the part of people who develop new inventions in order to obtain a monopolistic patent, although as of 1999 those new inventions may be for relatively small matters, rather than for new forms of transportation, communication, energy, or health care.

Changing the system by shortening the patent monopoly, requiring licensing, or having the government as an insurer against product liability can be helpful, but not as much as well-placed subsidies to encourage needed inventions.

Table 18-1. The Patent System and Encouraging Inventions

Criteria Alternatives	C Taxes and Profits	L Competition
C Preserve Patents	+	—
L Abolish Patents	—	+
N Change System	0	0
SOS 1. Well-Placed Subsidies to Encourage Technology 2. Licensing on Royalties 3. Government as Insurer	++	++

Well-placed subsidies could mean calling a conference of leading scientists and engineers to develop a list of 50-100 important needed inventions. The government could then announce the availability of grants and other monetary rewards to encourage the development of those inventions. The rewards could be worth more than a monopolistic patent, while still encouraging competition (rather than stifling it).

II. Alternatives for Product Liability

Common law defenses enable manufacturers to escape liability by arguing (1) they did not sell directly to the consumer, (2) contributor negligence by the consumer, (3) third party partially responsible, and (4) implicit waiver of the right to sue.

Strict liability means the manufacturer is liable for damages to the consumer if the product injured the consumer, regardless of the above common law defenses.

Comparative negligence means the consumer collects even if the consumer is partly negligent, as long as the part is less than 50%.

The SOS alternative as mentioned here provides for strict liability only after three years of marketing in order to stimulate product innovation and provide a time period for debugging product defects. A better SOS alternative might be to have the government be an insurer for the first three years so as to provide better compensation to injured persons while freeing product innovators from liability if they exercise reasonable care. See Table 18-2.

Table 18-2. Product Liability

Goals Alternatives	C Stimulate Innovation of Products	L Safety and Compensation
C Common Law Defenses	+	—
L Strict Liability	—	+
N Common Law Defenses with Exceptions or Comparative Negligence	0	0
SOS OR WIN-WIN Strict Liability after 3 Years of Marketing	++	++

III. Stimulating Socially Useful Research

The SOS emphasizes socializing people at an early age to want to discover new and useful knowledge. That means an emphasis on creativity and usefulness in elementary and secondary education.

Doing so is likely to result in more socially useful research than either pure market forces or making subsidies available, although such socialization can be combined with the stimulus of a free market and the facilitating value of a well-placed subsidy. See Table 18-3.

IV. Validity and Simplicity in Policy Analysis

Validity in policy analysis refers to internal consistency in drawing a prescriptive conclusion from goals, alternatives, and relations. It also refers to external consistency between the alleged goals, alternatives, and relations on the one hand and empirical reality on the other.

Simplicity in policy analysis refers to having as few goals, alternatives, and relations as are needed to capture the essence of the policy problem. Simplicity also includes an emphasis on simple arithmetic rather than calculus, operations research, or statistical analysis if possible.

Frequently policy analysts think of increasing validity by decreasing simplicity, or increasing simplicity by decreasing validity. The approach of using a decision matrix or an SOS table may provide greater validity by including goals that are normally difficult to work with using complex methods. Such goals may, however, be relatively easy to work with if simple methods are used that allow for a substantial margin of error. See Table 18-4.

Table 18-3. Socially Useful Research

Goals Alternatives	C 1. Freedom 2. Save Taxes	L 1. Usefulness
C 1. Laissez-Faire Encouraging What is Easy	+	—
L 1. Big Funding for Causal Research 2. Policy Research	—	+
N 1. Both	0	0
SOS OR WIN-WIN 1. Socialization with Free Market 2. Subsidies	++	++

Table 18-4. Validity And Simplicity

Goals Alternatives	C Proper Form	L Democratic Understanding
C Validity	+	—
L Simplicity	—	+
N 2 and 2	0	0
SOS OR WIN-WIN Striving for 100% on Both	++	++

V. Generalizations Versus Case Studies in Developing Knowledge

Generalizations versus case studies is a controversial issue in the developing of new knowledge, but those two concepts do not lend themselves to conservative and liberal labels. Liberals tend to emphasize induction since it is normally associated with empirical observation. Conservatives tend to emphasize deduction since it is normally associated with reasoning from authoritative axioms.

The two key purposes of developing new knowledge are for better causal understanding and for broad practical knowledge. Those goals are also difficult to associate with the labels of conservative or liberal. Business conservatives emphasize practical knowledge. Intellectual liberals emphasize causal understanding. Within the same scholarly discipline, however, conservatives may advocate knowledge for knowledge sake. The liberals may then advocate knowledge that has implications for public policy or practical affairs.

Regardless whether the alternatives and goals are labeled conservative, liberal, position #1, or position #2, the SOS alternative might be a cyclical approach. Case studies lead to generalizations, but then generalizations are applied to specific situations which add to the case studies including the exceptions to the generalizations. Those new case studies reinforce or modify the generalizations, which then get applied to new case situations, and so on. The result is likely to better causal understanding than just relying on generalizations, and simultaneously better practical knowledge than just relying on case studies. See Table 18-5.

Table 18-5. Generalizations Versus Case Studies

Goals Alternatives	C Causal Understanding	L Broad Practical Knowledge
C Generalizations	+	—
L Case Studies	—	+
N Middle Range	0	0
SOS OR WIN-WIN Cyclical Approach	++	++

Chapter 19

INTEGRATING INNOVATION IDEAS

This is the fourth in a series of articles dealing with government innovation in *Creativity Plus*. The first article appeared in the Spring 2000 issue and dealt with "Win-Win Performance Pay." The examples included:

1. Paying stock brokers a percentage of the dividends and/or resale profits.
2. Giving manufacturers an incentive to adopt cleaner processes by making those processes more profitable.
3. Paying employment agencies commissions after welfare recipients have been on the job for at least a few months.
4. Providing bonuses to police officers based on percentage of crimes solved by police units and individual officers.

The second article appeared in the Summer 2000 issue and dealt with "Win-Win Vouchers." The examples included:

1. Vouchers to cover the difference between a sub-minimum wage and a minimum wage, provided that the employer offers on-the-job training to bring the worker up to at least the minimum wage level.
2. Vouchers to cover the difference between what workers can afford to pay for food and what farmers need to supply the food, provided that both the workers and the farmers upgrade their productivity.
3. Housing vouchers to get inner-city residents to move up one concentric circle in economic neighborhoods so that their children will go to better schools.
4. Training vouchers to be used by any adult to upgrade his or her productivity through training, but the vouchers cannot be redeemed unless the trainee passes a test and can be redeemed in double if the trainee obtains a new job for at least six months.

The third article appeared in the Autumn 2000 issue and dealt with "Win-Win Contracting Out." The examples included:

1. Contracting out state factories or state farms with provisions for protecting workers, consumers, and the environment or else the contract is terminated or not renewed.

2. Contracting out legal services for the poor with provisions for law reform activities, clarifying and enforcing existing rights, affirmative recruitment, public education, seeking legislation, law school interaction, and the writing of the appropriate articles and books.
3. Contracting out prisons with specifications that they should be operated at 80% of former cost and the recidivism rate should be improved by at least 10%.
4. Contracting out some or all of the public schools with provisions requiring cost reduction rather than production, test score improvement, and integration.

The purpose of this article is to provide further illustrations of win-win performance pay, vouchers, and contracting out.

I. More Win-Win Performance Pay: Health

The additional example of win-win performance pay relates to the use of health management organizations (HMO's) as a key part of healthcare policy.

Medicare and Medicaid emphasize individuals who go to whatever doctor will service them, and then the government pays all or a high percentage of each case-by-case doctor bill. Such a system tends to be much more expensive than salaried government doctors and is inequitable if it only covers the poor and the aged.

Government-owned hospitals or salaried government doctors tend to be inefficient due to lack of competition. Such a system is also inequitable if it only applies to veterans or poor people since health care expenses can no longer be easily afforded by lower middle-class people or middle-class people in general.

Subsidized HMO's in this context means the government provides health care vouchers to poor people, aged people, and middle-class people who can qualify. Such vouchers supplement the premiums which HMO's require in order to provide HMO coverage. The HMO's compete with each other, thereby generating lower prices and better quality service. The money for the vouchers can come mainly from employers to cover their own employees, with a provision for covering the self-employed and the non-employed. See Table 1.

II. More Win-Win Vouchers: Schools

When people think of vouchers in the school policy context, they think of vouchers that will support parochial and private schools at the expense of public schools. This is not necessarily the case.

Privatization can be either conservative if private companies are paid to achieve conservative goals, or it can be liberal if private companies are paid to achieve liberal goals.

Table 2 shows the school vouchers situation in a win-win context. Conservatives tend to favor vouchers for elementary and high school. Doing so will save taxpayer money by diverting students away from the public schools with private and parochial schools absorbing some of the costs. Such schools will also be more disciplined.

Liberals object to vouchers for elementary and high schools. They argue in favor of using the money for inner-city public schools. Their goal is to improve inner-city learning and to preserve the public school system.

A win-win voucher system might provide for government vouchers to attend non-governmental schools including those that may be run by the parochial school system. If they are run by the parochial school system, they must be in buildings that have no religious orientation such as crucifixes on the walls. The teachers must also be either non-priests or non-nuns or possibly some priests and nuns wearing secular clothing.

Such a system could be a win-win system. It would save taxpayer money especially if the secular schools run by the parochial school systems agree to a tuition rate per student that is less than what it costs per student to educate them in the public school system. While getting costs down, the learning quality could go up as a result of (1) more experienced teachers who are willing to teach in the inner-city schools, (2) salaries based on performance rather than union seniority, and (3) a more disciplined atmosphere. Those learning quality factors could appeal to both conservatives and liberals especially when there is no breach of separation of church and state as there would be in vouchers to parochial schools.

Table 1. Healthcare Policy

Goals **Alternatives**	**C** **Privatization**	**L** **Equity**
C Marketplace or Medicare + and Medicaid	+	–
L Government-owned hospitals	–	+
N Both	0	0
SOS OR WIN-WIN Subsidized HMO's	++	++

Table 2. Vouchers for Secular-Parochial Schools

Goals Alternatives	C 1. Save taxpayer money 2. More disciplined schools	L Improve inner-city education learning
C Vouchers for elementary and high schools	+	–
L No vouchers for elementary and high schools Using the money for inner-city public schools	–	+
SOS OR WIN-WIN Vouchers for secular inner-city schools run by the parochial school system	++	++

III. MORE WIN-WIN CONTRACTING OUT: SOLID WASTE

Conservatives tend to favor privatization in sold waste collection, in order to increase individual responsibility and reduce taxes. Liberals tend to favor government collection with recycling, in order to increase community responsibility and provide for a cleaner environment.

A compromise is to provide for contracting out by the city government. That is better from a conservative viewpoint than solid waste collection by government employees, but not so good as having each residence or business arrange for solid waste collection. Contracting out is better from a liberal viewpoint than total privatization because the government is in control of who will get the contract and what the contract provisions will be more than if the government tries to regulate the solid waste collectors, but not as much as the government doing the collecting itself.

An SOS solution would be one that reduces the cost of the contract and provides for an even cleaner environment by preventing the solid waste form coming into existence or needing collection. That can be done by giving homeowners and businesses vouchers to buy various kinds of equipment and services that will reduce the need for solid waste collection. An example would be a voucher for buying a mulcher for one's lawnmower to reduce the need for grass collection. Another example would be a voucher for buying a tin-can compactor, which substantially reduces the cost and expense of collecting and recycling tin cans.

The 1994 experience of Champaign indicates that regulated privatization may be more of an SOS alternative than contracting out. The regulation requires private haulers to pick up recyclables. If recycling is purely voluntary, it does not get done so well. The regulation also requires every business firm and household to arrange for hauling of garbage and recyclables. That is a mix of liberal regulation with private enterprise doing the work. The government is in control, but the contracting out is by business firms and households.

Table 3. Solid Waste Collection

Goals / Alternatives	C **1. Individual responsibility** **2. Reduce taxes**	L **1. Community responsibility** **2. Clean environment**
C 1. Privatization	+	–
L 1. Government collection with recycling	–	+
N 1. Contracting out	0	0
SOS OR WIN-WIN 1. Vouchers to reduce solid waste 2. Contracting out	++	++

IV. Some Conclusions

This series of four articles has illustrated that win-win performance pay, win-win vouchers, and win-win contracting out can be a useful form of government innovation. They are useful in the sense that they are geared toward enabling both conservatives and liberals to come out ahead of their best initial expectations simultaneously. Ordinary performance pay, vouchers, and contracting out tend to be geared more toward conservative privatization, especially with regard to contracting out, or toward liberal vouchers which may be a form of welfare handouts, like food stamps. Performance pay tends to be either conservative or liberal depending on whether people are being paid to perform conservative or liberal goals.

As part of our desire to get readers of *Creativity Plus* more involved in an interactive way with this journal of the Policy Studies Organization, we would like to invite readers to suggest other forms of win-win performance pay, win-win vouchers, and win-win contracting out. There may be many more government activities and goals that could benefit from this kind of useful innovation, but the applications have not been made or even suggested. These are new and useful ways of thinking about governmental activity. If two heads are better than one, then 1,200 PSO thinkers should be better than two, without too many cooks spoiling the chicken soup for the creative soul.

SECTION B: DISPUTE RESOLUTION

Chapter 20

WIN-WIN MEDIATION

I. GENERAL

The conservative alternative in most civil litigation is for the defendant to win on trial. The defendant is usually an insurance company or some other type of business firm. The liberal alternative is generally for the plaintiff to win on trial. The plaintiff is usually someone who has been injured (1) in an automobile accident, (2) on the job, or (3) in an accident involving a consumer product. The neutral alternative is a compromise settlement between what the plaintiff is asking and what the defendant is offering.

The criteria for deciding which alternative is best include benefits to the defendant, benefits to the plaintiff, costs to the defendant, and costs to the plaintiff. The conservative alternative does well on the conservative totals, with higher weight to the conservative goals. The liberal alternative does well on the liberal totals, with higher weight to the liberal goals.

The object is to develop an alternative whereby both the plaintiff and defendant can come out ahead of their best initial expectations simultaneously. Such an alternative may involve the defendant giving the plaintiff valuable insurance or other products. Such products may be worth a lot to the plaintiff in terms of market prices. They may, however, have only a relatively small cost to the defendant when they are products that the defendant manufactures or sells. See Table 1.

II. PRODUCT LIABILITY

Table 2 on super-optimizing litigation analysis illustrates an approach to mediating super-optimum solutions. It is called big benefits for one side and low costs for the other. SOS solutions enable plaintiffs, defendants, conservatives, liberals, and other major viewpoints to all come out ahead of their best initial expectations simultaneously. Such solutions are facilitated by spreadsheet-based decision-aiding software. Table 2 illustrates this analysis using *Traveller's Insurance v. Sanyo Electronics* as a specific illustrative example.

The subject matter of the case was product liability. Traveller's Insurance paid out more than $900,000 in fine loss claims supposedly due to a defective combustible Sanyo tape deck.

Traveller's sued to be reimbursed. The case can be used especially to indicate how win-win mediation can facilitate super-optimum settlements.

Table 1. Win-Win Mediation in General

Goals Alternatives	C Benefits to defendant	L Benefits to plaintiff
C Defendant wins on expensive trial	+	-
L Plaintiff wins on expensive trial	-	+
N Settle	0	0
SOS OR WIN-WIN For example insurance or products from the defendant	++	++

Table 2 illustrates what is involved in this super-optimum settlement. The plaintiff demands $700,000 as a minimum in order to settle. The defendant offers $300,000 as a maximum in order to settle. The object of a super-optimum settlement is to provide the plaintiff with more than $700,000 while simultaneously not having the defendant pay more than $300,000. In other words, the problem is to find a number that is simultaneously bigger than $700,000 and smaller than $300,000, which are roughly the best expectations of the plaintiff and defendant respectively.

Such a settlement can be arrived at by considering additional settlement criteria beyond the exchange of money. In almost every damages case, the defendant is an insurance company, a manufacturer, a transportation company, or some other kind of company that can offer something of considerable value to the plaintiff, but having relatively low cost to the defendant. In this case, it was possible for the defendant to consider offering electronic equipment, insurance claims, and insurance annuities to the plaintiffs and their insurance companies. The claims were held by Sanyo's Japanese insurance company against Americans, but not considered worth pursuing by the Japanese company, although of considerable value to the U. S. insurance company. That combination of equipment, claims, and annuities had an estimated cost value of only $226,000 to the defendant, as indicated by Table 2. The package, however, had an estimated purchase value of $1,099,000 to the plaintiff.

Table 2. The Sanyo Product-Liability Case

Goals Alternatives	C Pro defendant (pay as little as possible)	L Pro plaintiff (receive as much as possible)
C Defendant's initial offer = $300,000.	+	-
L Plaintiff's initial demand = $700,000	-	+
N Likely compromise settlement = $500,000	0	0
SOS OR WIN-WIN 1. Computers from defendant to plaintiff. 2. Big screen TVs from defendant to plaintiff. 3. Insurance claims from defendant to plaintiff.	Worth less than $300,00 to defendant ++	Worth more than $700,000 to plaintiff ++

The solution that was suggested to the Sanyo case by the mediators and reacted to seriously by the Japanese side was:

1. The Japanese insurance company sells marine insurance as one of its specialities, but sells almost no marine insurance in the United States, but only to Asian shipping companies.
2. There are, however, a lot of shipping companies in the United States. They include shipping companies that fly the Panama flag or the Liberia flag, but are owned by Americans. They fly those flags for the same reason that many corporations incorporate in Delaware, namely, to decrease regulation.
3. The Japanese insurance company was willing to bring the Traveller's Insurance Company in on a deal. The Traveller's Insurance Company would become the agent for selling marine insurance in the United States. The expected sales might be as much as $10 million a year, with about $5 million to go to Traveller's Insurance, and $5 million to the Japanese insurance company.

That kind of settlement would put the American insurance company ahead $5 million a year into the future although that would be a gross figure with some expenses involved. The Japanese insurance company would be $5 million ahead every year as a result of sales it would not otherwise be making. That is a much better solution and gets much more out of the realm of the idea that the defendant gives and the plaintiff receives. This is emphasizing that both receive.

The reasons it did not work were:

1. The law firm representing the Traveller's Insurance Company is one of the biggest in the United States, and the lawyers representing the firm were among the top litigation lawyers in the insurance business. Yet their minds were so channeled along traditional thinking that they could not conceive of anything other than money coming from the defendant to the plaintiff. It was a mental block situation in part.
2. There was also quite possibly a violation of legal ethics in that the Traveller's Insurance Company's law firm was thinking of its own interests more than the interests of its client, and thinking very shortsightedly. Any package arrangement would have to be worked out between the law firm and Traveller's Insurance as to how the law firm would get paid. The law firm was not willing to wait for a percentage of $5 million a year. They wanted cash now. The cash now, though, could have been provided by Traveller's without it being a percentage of a damage payment. The representative from Traveller's, though, was a bit browbeaten by his own attorney. He did not exercise independent judgment, but just went along with his attorney. The deal required some good business sense and not legalistic lawyer sense.
3. A solution involving a mutually beneficial business arrangement is definitely more complicated than merely writing a check. It would require people being present from the marine insurance aspects of the Japanese firm, and people being present from Traveller's Insurance who might be involved in selling the marine insurance. No such people were present, at least on the Traveller's Insurance side. The person who was present seemed to have little authority, and he seemed to be unwilling to exercise whatever authority he did have. The person on the Japanese side seemed to have more authority, though there were some language problems. He also seemed agreeable (although this may have reflected a cultural and personality difference), as he appeared to be more willing to listen.

III. Labor-Management

The illustrative example that follows involves a leading grower in the Peoria, Illinois, area (who employs approximately 7,000 farm workers a year) being sued by the Migrant Legal Counsel, which is a legal services agency that specializes in the legal problems of migratory farm workers.

The plaintiff's wildest initial expectation is to be repaid approximately $1 million in wages. That is a wild expectation since the money was deducted for goods, services, and advances that had been provided to the workers by the grower, but not in accordance with the proper paperwork procedures.

The defendant's wildest initial expectation is to have to pay nothing. That is a wild expectation since the defendant admittedly failed to comply with the proper deduction procedures with no good defense other than that the money was owed. The defendant would thus be likely to lose on the issue of whether they complied with the proper procedures. A penalty is likely to be assessed to deter such improprieties on the part of the specific defendant and other potential defendants. The penalty is likely to be substantial in order to have deterrent value. There is also likely to be compensation to the named defendants for their efforts plus considerable litigation costs if the case goes to trial.

The object is thus to arrive at a super-optimum solution whereby the workers in a sense receive more than $1 million and the defendant pays less than nothing.

The key element in the super-optimum solution is the establishment of a credit union mainly consisting of $100,000 from the defendant to be deposited with interest for five years.

That $100,000 can quickly generate $2 million worth of housing by serving as a 10% down payment on a mortgage for existing or new housing units for the workers. The housing might be used as collateral for additional capital. It is also possible that a federal or state government agency will match the $1 million as part of an economic development plan, thereby further increasing the lending opportunities.

The workers thereby obtain multiple family housing and a lending source for business opportunities that may be worth at least $2 million plus the benefits of an improved grievance procedure, payments to named plaintiffs, and compliance information. The total value is worth more than their wildest best expectation.

Table 3. The Ramirez Labor-Management Case

Goals **Alternatives**	**C** **Little money to plaintiff**	**L** **Big money to plaintiff**
C Defendant's best expectation = $0	+	-
L Plaintiff's best expectation = $1,000,000	-	+
N Likely compromise settlement = $500,000	0	0
SOS OR WIN-WIN 1. Credit union, housing, and business opportunities 2. Grievance procedures 3. Payment to named plaintiff 4. Compliance information 5. Thus, big benefits for plaintiff and low cost to defendant	++	++

The growers thereby obtain the benefits of not having to provide housing for the workers. They also get interest on their savings and a subsequent return of the principal if requested. The grievance procedures can decrease friction. The compliance information can increase credibility. Payment to the named plaintiffs is a cost rather than a benefit, but it is more than offset by the benefits from the other relevant items of value. Therefore the growers are making a net gain as a result of this SOS settlement which is the same as paying less than nothing.

IV. Some Lessons

One moral of the story (or the bottom line of the analysis) is that what has been referred to as an SOS may be relatively small thinking compared to what could be developed in SOS dispute resolution. We do not have a concept yet that involves a higher level of dispute resolution than super-optimum.

1. Pareto optimum solutions involve all sides holding constant to where they had previously been, and at least one side moving up one notch. That is not very optimum.
2. Compromise solutions are optimum only in a semantic or psychological way. They may really be lose-lose situations. They are basically everybody coming out ahead of their worst expectations, meaning everybody could lose big, but they think they might have lost even bigger.
3. In an SOS, everybody comes out ahead of their best expectations, which sounds good. It is, however, still a relative concept dependent on the thinking that initially goes into what constitutes best expectations.
4. In a zero-sum solution, what one side gives up the other side gains. Thus, the sum of the pluses and minuses add to zero. In a non-zero-sum solution or an expanded-sum solution, one side may gain more than the other side loses. That is closely related to an SOS with a product exchange. The maker of the product gives up less in his dollar-loss value than the receiver of the product receives in terms of his dollar-gain value.
5. We need a concept (like positive benefits to all) that gets across the idea that all sides could positively gain in an absolute sense and not just relative to their worst or best expectations. In other words, in the Sanyo case, if the defendant expects at his initial lowest to pay $300,000 in damages and litigation expenses, but only paid $100,000, that would still be a $100,000 loss or negative cost. The marine insurance deal involves a positive gain to both the defendant and the plaintiff.

The SOS may actually not even satisfy Pareto optimally because one side does give up something, and thus that side comes out behind in an absolute sense from where it started. If Sanyo gives up a penny, then that is not a Pareto optimum solution even if the plaintiff gets a trillion dollars. It should not make any difference whether it is Pareto optimum since Pareto optimally is such a perversion of common sense. Virtually no one would say that in the following situation, Pareto solution A is better than non-Pareto solution B. Solution A involves one penny to the plaintiffs and nothing taken away from the defendant because maybe the government pays the penny to the plaintiff. That is a Pareto optimum. Under solution B, the defendant gives up the penny and the plaintiffs become a million dollars richer. That would be considered unacceptable under Pareto optimally. It is an ideological orientation that is opposed to the rich giving up anything on behalf of the collective good.

The SOS-plus concept we are referring to is one in which all sides positively gain. One thing that complicates this situation is applying it to litigation as contrasted to applying it to other kinds of disputes, such as policy disputes. In litigation, one has a plaintiff who is suing for damages (i.e., asking for dollars), and one has a defendant who is generally saying you are asking for too much. I will give you less than what you are asking for if you will agree to sign a release and stop suing. That kind of thinking inherently throws the whole problem into an at least partly negative solution.

The proposed situation though should be distinguished from a situation where the defendant proposes to the plaintiff that they join together in a kind of conspiracy against others. An example would be where the defendant insurance company and the plaintiff insurance company agree that they will work together to wipe out other insurance companies, to artificially raise prices to the detriment of the people buying insurance or to decrease the services they provide. By agreeing to such an agreement, both companies may come out ahead. The concept of superoptimality though needs to consider the effect on third parties, such as consumers or other companies.

It is worthwhile to get people in a super-optimum solution frame of mind by emphasizing that we are looking for mutually beneficial solutions and not compromises. Perhaps someday this win-win reasoning process will have become incorporated into commonplace negotiation behavior.

V. Win-Win Mediation

1. Compromise Mediation: Both sides partially lose, but they console themselves by saying that it could have been worse.
2. Pareto Optimum Mediation: Neither side loses, but neither side may win anything substantial.
3. Third-party Mediation: Generally a compromise, but the mediator gets well paid.
4. Non-Zero Sum Game Mediation: All sides can lose except one whose gains more than offset the losses.
5. Lose-Lose Mediation: Both sides wind up substantial losers in view of the expenses of mediation and in view of the opportunity costs.
6. Win-Lose Mediation: One side wins and the other side loses, but the dispute has been ended or resolved.
7. Win-Win Mediation: All major sides win beyond their best expectations with or without a third party mediator.
8. Win-Win Negotiation: All major sides compete to see who can come up with the best win-win solution, but without a third party mediator.
9. Super-Optimizing Mediation: A synonym for win-win mediation.

For further details on win-win mediation, see "Multi-Criteria Dispute Resolution" in Nagel, *Policy Analysis Methods and Super-Optimum Solutions* (Nova Science, 1994). For earlier background, see "Resolving Rule-Applying, Litigation, and Related Disputes" in

Nagel and Miriam Mills, *Multi-Criteria Methods for Alternative Dispute Resolution: With Microcomputer Software Applications* (Greenwood-Quorum, 1990). For more recent applications, see "Computer-Aided Mediation" in Nagel, *Computer-Aided Judicial Analysis: Predicting, Prescribing, and Administering* (Greenwood-Quorum, 1992).

Chapter 21

Promoting Democracy

Part One: Political Representation and Electoral Reform

The conservative *alternative* to voting rights in South Africa has been to deny blacks the right to vote. The extreme left-wing alternative of some of the Pan-Africans has been to deny whites the right to vote, or even to expel them from the country, meaning deny that they have any right to even live in South Africa. The middling position is everybody has one person, one vote, although that could be considered a left-wing position since the blacks would dominate.

The black *goal* is basically for blacks to be better off. The white goal is not necessarily for whites to be better off than they presently are, but to at least not be much worse off.

The conservative position and the more extreme left-wing position would *result* in a kind of super-malimum position where both blacks and whites would be worse off.

1. The only way the conservatives could succeed in keeping blacks from having the right to vote any longer would be through a system of repression even greater than they have attempted in the past. The country would be in a state of continuous guerrilla warfare with no security from being bombed or assassinated. There would be no foreign business, or not much that would want to locate there. Much domestic business would leave.
2. If the extreme blacks had their way and all the whites were driven out, the result would be somewhat similar in that there would be a lack of foreign investment. Much domestic business would leave voluntarily or involuntarily.

Table 21-1. Voting Rights in South Africa

Alternatives / Goals	CONS Whites well off	LIB Blacks well off
CONS Only whites vote	+	-
LIB 1. Only blacks vote 2. Majority rule without minority safeguards	-	+
NEUTRAL 1. Bill of rights: Free speech, equal treatment, due process 2. U.S. Constitution: Senate, electoral college, special majorities to pass, amend	0	0
SOS OR WIN-WIN Economic rights: Economic growth, upgraded skills combined with neutral alternatives.	++	++

The *object* is to develop a system in which none of those bad things happen, meaning:

1. Foreign investment does not shy away from South Africa, but substantially increases.
2. Businesses within South Africa stay there and even expand to hire more people and make for more job opportunities.
3. Violence ends as contrasted to merely being temporarily suspended as the situation is now, waiting to see what will happen.

The compromise position is not really one person, one vote. That is the non-extreme left-wing position. The *extreme* left-wing position is no voting rights to whites at all. At least at the present time, the conservative position is not to deny blacks access to jobs, public accommodations, schools, etc. The conservative position is to wipe out all apartheid and all segregation except for voting rights. The *extreme conservative* position is to preserve all apartheid and segregation.

The *compromise* position is one person, one vote but some kind of guarantee that whites will not be outvoted in spite of the fact that they have so much fewer people. The proposed devices are:

1. Partition the country into states like the United States, especially as of the 13 states. Every state no matter how small gets two senators. There would be basically four states in South Africa, namely the Cape provinces, Natal, Transvaal, and the Orange Free State. The first two would be black, the last two could be dominated by Afrikaans. There would be not eight senators. Maybe each state would have five

senators so there would be 20 senators. But the blacks could not run the Senate any more than the north could run the U.S. Senate. The white states would have the power to prevent even ordinary legislation from being passed, but especially any legislation that requires a 2/3 vote like the approval of treaties or appointments and any amendments to the constitution would require a 3/4 vote.

2. Everything that has been proposed is exactly what was adopted in the United States in the constitution. There would be separation of powers, federalism, judicial review. Everything designed to enable a minority of states to be able to prevent the majority from exercising the power that its numbers have. They would have an electoral college in which the president would be chosen on the basis of how many senators each state has, which would have nothing to do with how many people they have since every state would have the same number of senators. They would have a supreme court that would have the power to declare unconstitutional legislation that interferes with property rights, state's rights, all of which would be code words for white people's rights.
3. It is ironic that those who want to preserve white power in South Africa choose as their model the American constitution, including the Bill of Rights. They are all of a sudden very much in favor of minority rights because they are the minority. Here the word minority means numerical minority, not lacking in power.

A super-optimum solution would have to involve something that would be the equivalent of an internal economic union. It would have to involve a system whereby white business interests would have an environment in which they could prosper, and blacks would have job opportunities accompanied by merit criteria, affirmative action with preferences for people who cannot satisfy a minimum competence level. It basically means going directly to what it is that each side wants to achieve by way of increased voting power and concentrating on how to more than guarantee that regardless of the voting rights. It means elevating certain economic rights to a higher status than the status of federalism, separation of powers, and those other constitutional issues.

The key way out is to emphasize both blacks and whites being much better of economically as a result of SOS thinking. That is, political power is directed toward economic well-being for each group.

A key thing is to get away from stability toward continuous economic growth and to get into responsiveness in regard to upgrading skills rather than forming a new government. Making those rights meaningful includes a right to sue but also the establishment of appropriate institutions like a ministry of international trade and industry. I had overemphasized the right to sue, although that can be part of it.

There are three responses or questions or types of questions that can be asked of revolutionary South African blacks:

1. What is going to happen to the whites? That is an implicitly racist question that shows rather biased sensitivity to what is going to happen to the whites but not what is going to happen to the blacks who may be in bad shape as a result of white flight, loss of investment, and other socio-economic disruptions.
2. How to get whites and blacks to make concessions? That is the traditional compromise position, which is better than civil war.

3. The SOS question is how to enable both blacks and whites to be better off than their best expectations? The SOS dispute resolution activity is one that we are getting increasingly involved with.

PART TWO: NEGOTIATING FACULTY SALARIES

This example was developed at People's University and Beijing University especially by Professor King Chow and a graduate student named Lu Junwei. The example involves the dispute between the government and university professors in China over faculty salaries.

The professors have been seeking a salary of approximately 300 Yuan for a certain time period. The government has been willing to give at the most 200 Yuan. The object is to come up with a way in which the faculty members could be paid more than 300 Yuan, but where the government would be able to pay even less than 200 Yuan.

The solution developed by Professor Chow, Mr. Lu, and others, is to institute a system of low tuition throughout the Chinese universities while simultaneously increasing the number of eligible students. The money obtained could be used to pay faculty salary increases without having to draw upon the government's limited resources. Provision could be made for low-income students to receive scholarships or loans, especially loans that would be forgiven if the students go into fields of work that are in short supply. The result would be salaries higher than 300 Yuan for faculty, with a possible reduction of the government's contribution to less than 200 Yuan. The result would also be more people receiving college educations to the benefit of national productivity which in turn would bring in increased national income and more government revenue. These various relations are summarized in Table 21-2.

Table 21-2. Evaluating Policies Concerning Chinese Faculty Salaries

Goals Alternatives	CONS Decrease cost of government	LIB Attract faculty
CONS Government offer	+	-
LIB Faculty demand	-	+
NEUTRAL Compromise	0	0
SOS OR WIN-WIN Tuition and scholarships	++	++

Note: Neutral goals on minimum constraints supported by both conservatives and liberals include (1) having an educated population, (2) having a high national income, (3) having public policy that is politically feasible, and (4) equity to students.

This is an example of a super-optimum solution where everyone comes out ahead. The low faculty salaries have also been a point of antagonism between the government and graduate students who anticipate becoming professors, especially when sellers of orange pop and cucumbers can make more in a few days than a university faculty member makes in a month.

The Chinese faculty salaries problem thus illustrates such broader aspects of public policy evaluation as:

1. Having a third-party benefactor is a useful way of arriving at super-optimum solutions, but the third-party benefactor does not have to be the government. That is especially so when the government is one of the two main parties. In this context, the third-party benefactor was in effect the students paying tuition.
2. The importance of considering the side effects of an SOS solution on the gross national product. Those side effects include (1) the multiplier effect which occurs as a result of increased income causing increased income for numerous other people via a chain of spending, (2) the compound interest effect which occurs from an increase in the base to which next year's growth rates are applied similar to getting compound interest on interest, (3) the inter-generational effect as a result of improving parental role models, (4) the taxpaying feedback effect due to the increased GNP generating more tax money and subsidy money even if the tax rate is constant or lowered, (5) the export surplus effect which occurs via a productivity surplus that is available for export to obtain new capital goods and technologies which further increase productivity, and (6) the welfare reduction effect whereby the prosperity of an increased GNP means less of a burden on the government to provide for unemployment compensation, public aid, public housing, food stamps, Medicaid, and other forms of welfare. These six points emphasize the upward-spiral benefits of investing in human resources and new technologies for increasing the gross national product.
3. The importance of considering equity and not just effectiveness and efficiency in evaluating alternative public policies. It is ironic that equity may be more considered in an affluent capitalistic society than in a hard-pressed Marxist society, even though Marxism in theory is supposed to be more sensitive to the spread of benefits and costs across economic classes and ethnic groups.

Chapter 22

WIN-WIN PEACE NEGOTIATIONS

I. SUPER POWER AND A QUASI COLONIAL NATION

Developing nations may not be as involved with private international law as more industrialized nations are. Private international law refers to the rules governing business transactions that involve citizens or key facts from different countries. Developing nations may have more need for public international law than developed nations do. Public international law refers to the rules concerning government-to-government relations. The more industrialized countries may be able to resolve their disputes through negotiation without resorting to an international tribunal. The less developed countries with less bargaining power may have more need for international tribunals, as was the case in Nicaragua obtaining an injunction from the International Court of Justice against the mining of its harbors by the United States.

Developing nations may also have international law problems with former colonial powers seeking to maintain a possibly unwanted military presence in the new nation. This is partly the case with the American military bases in the Philippines. The legal and policy problems of those bases may be a fitting way to conclude this paper since they are especially challenging problems, although so are the other previously discussed problems. All these problems in order to qualify as SOS problems need to have the following characteristics:

1. There should be at least one conservative alternative and at least one liberal alternative. If there is only one alternative for dealing with the problem, then there is no problem since there is no choice, although one could say that there is still a go/no-go choice as to whether that one alternative should be adopted.
2. There should be at least one conservative and at least one liberal goal. If all the goals are conservative, then the conservative alternative should easily win. Likewise if all the goals are liberal, then the liberal alternative should easily win,
3. The conservative alternative should do better on the conservative goal, with the liberal alternative doing better on the liberal goal. That is the tradeoff requirement. If either alternative does better on both kinds of goals, then that alternative should easily win.
4. It should be possible to meaningfully say that conservatives give relatively more weight to the conservative goals and relatively less weight to the liberal goals, and

vice versa for the assigning of weights by liberals. If that is not so, then it is not so meaningful to talk about a conservative total with conservative weights and a liberal total with liberal weights.

5. There should be a super-optimum solution that does better than the previous conservative alternative on the conservative totals with conservative weights, and it also does better than the previous liberal alternative on the liberal totals with liberal weights. That is the most difficult to achieve of these five characteristics, but still manageable.

The problem of what to do about the American military bases in the Philippines is especially difficult because it goes beyond the usual dilemma of choosing between (1) a liberal alternative that clearly wins with liberal weights, and (2) a conservative alternative that clearly wins with conservative weights. An analysis of Table 22-1 tends to show that the liberal alternative barely squeaks by the conservative and neutral alternatives on the liberal totals, and the conservative alternative barely squeaks by the other two alternatives on the conservative totals. We thus have an even tighter than usual dilemma between the liberal and conservative alternatives.

Table 22-1. The Philippine-U.S. Military Bases

Criteria Alternatives	CONS Conservative Concerns C=3 L=1	LIB Liberal Concerns L=3 C=1	LIB Sovereignty L=3 C=1	NEUTRAL Total Neutral Weights	CONS Total Conservative Weights	LIB Total Liberal Weights
CONS Bases and more money	4	3	2	18	17*	19
LIB No bases	2	3	4	18	13	23*
NEUTRAL Phase out	3	3	2	16	14	18
SOS OR WIN-WIN Bases and massive credits to upgrade economy	5	6	3	26	23**	29**

A. The Alternatives

Working backward from those totals to the alternatives, the conservative alter-native is basically to allow the American bases to remain, but to ask for more money. The liberal alternative is to throw the bases out. The neutral alternative is something in between, generally a gradual phasing out of the bases. Other in-between positions might involve throwing out the Clark Air Base but keeping the Subic Naval Base, or vice versa. Another possibility is allow the bases but with more flying of Philippine flags at the bases and other symbols of Philippine sovereignty. A recent middling position is allow the bases, but give the

Philippine government more say in how the planes should be used, especially with regard to putting down an attempted coup.

The phasing out idea is probably the most common middling alternative. It, however, blends into both the conservative and the liberal alternatives. The conservatives are willing to tolerate the bases, but they are going to be eventually phased out to some extent anyhow as the cold war decreases even further. They are also going to be phased out to some extent because they have probably already become rather obsolete in light of modern defense technology. Few if any of the planes or ships could ever get anywhere without being destroyed by modern missiles. The Russian equivalent of nuclear-armed Trident submarines in the Pacific Ocean could probably wipe out both the naval base and the air base almost before the alarm could ring. There are also bases that are possibly more welcome in nearby Okinawa and Korea.

Likewise, the liberal alternative of throwing out the bases would have to be phased out. They cannot be thrown out within a matter of hours. For one thing, the liberal and conservative members of the Philippine House of Representatives would not tolerate a rushed departure without allowing for substitute employment opportunities and some substitution for the large amounts of money that are spent by Americans associated with the bases. The Philippine Senate is elected at large and is not so sensitive to Luzon constituency pressures where the bases are located.

One might therefore think there is really only one alternative here, namely phase out the bases. This problem, however, illustrates the importance of symbolism and language in political controversy. Whether the liberals really mean it or not, they talk about throwing out the bases now, not phasing them out. Whether the conservatives really mean it or not, they talk about retaining the bases indefinitely. Thus the controversy needs to be resolved in terms of what each side argues, not necessarily in terms of the realities beneath the surface. Perceptions, value judgments, and symbolism are often more important in resolving political controversies than empirical reality, especially in the short run.

B. The Goals

As for goals, Table 22-1 lists the first goal as "Liberal Concerns." That means a whole set of interests that liberals are especially sensitive to, including workers rather than employers, consumers rather than merchants, tenants rather than landlords, small farmers-businesses rather than big farmers-businesses, debtors rather than creditors, minority ethnic groups rather than dominant ethnic groups, and in general the relatively less well-off segments within society. The second goal is listed as "Conservative Concerns." That means a set of interests to which conservatives are especially sensitive, including employers, merchants, landlords, big farmers, big businesses, creditors, and dominant ethnic groups. One useful aspect of this problem is that it goes to the heart of liberal versus conservative interests and constituencies, as contrasted to lower impact problems.

The third goal is national sovereignty. In some contexts, that can be a conservative goal such as where Russia nationalists talk about restraining the Lithuanians, expelling the Jews, or otherwise discriminating against citizens of the Soviet Union who are not ethnic Russians. In other contexts, sovereignty can be a liberal left-wing goal, such as where Vietnamese advocate becoming sovereign from China, France, Japan, France again, the United States, and

China again during various points in Vietnamese history. Likewise it is a liberal concept in the Philippines when Filipinos talk about getting rid of the Spanish colonialists or the American Imperialists. including what they consider to be military-base imperialism. That makes sovereignty in this analysis a relatively liberal goal. Obviously the goal of conservative concerns is a conservative goal, and the goal of liberal concerns is a liberal one.

C. Scoring the Relations

As for scoring the relations of the alternatives on the goals, both the liberal and conservative concerns are to some extent favorably benefited by the present and additional American dollars. Those dollars benefit both workers and employers, consumers and merchants, tenants and landlords, small and large farmers, small and large businesses, debtors and creditors, and both minority and dominant ethnic groups. The amount of money is quite substantial. The Philippines is one of the top three recipients of American foreign aid in the world along with Israel and Egypt, whose aid is lessening. The liberal and conservative concerns, however, do not benefit equally. The American presence has a conservative influence. The United States tends to be supportive of conservative pro-American politicians, especially in a country that has American military bases like Korea, Greece, Turkey, West Germany, Spain, and the Philippines.

To be more specific, the conservative alternative of retaining the bases with even more money is a bit of a wash or a 3 on a 1-5 scale with regard to liberal concerns. The money is at least a 4 on liberal concerns, but the conservative influence of the United States is a 2 or lower. Those two sub-scores average a 3. On the conservative concerns, the conservative alternative of the bases and more money gets at least a 4 On sovereignty, the conservative alternative is at least a 2 on a 1-5 scale, which is the equivalent of a -1 on a -1 to +2 scale.

The liberal alternative also produces a washed-out 3 on liberal concerns. It gets a 4 with regard to getting rid of some of the American conservative influence, but it gets a 2 on losing the American money. The liberal alternative of no bases gets a 2 or lower on conservative concerns. It does relatively well on sovereignty, as both liberals and conservatives can recognize, although they may disagree on the relative weight of sovereignty in this context.

The neutral phase-out approach does about middling on liberal concerns. It provides some money for a while, which is good, but not as good as a lot of money for a long time. It provides a diminishing of American conservative Influence, but not as fast as the liberals would like, and not as slow as the conservatives might like. By allowing the Americans to retain the bases even under a phase-out arrangement, the neutral alternative does have a negative effect on Philippine sovereignty, although not as negative as the conservative alternative. We could show that difference by giving the neutral alternative a 2.5 on sovereignty or the conservative alternative a 1.5. Either way, the overall results are not affected.

D. A Super-Optimum Solution

Those overall results are that the liberal alternative wins on the liberal totals and the conservative alternative wins on the conservative totals although not by much, as previously mentioned. Finding a super-optimum solution may be especially difficult where the alternatives are so nearly tied and where the problem is so filled with emotional symbolism. A possible super-optimum solution would involve two key elements. The first is a recognition (as much as possible on all sides) that the bases are probably going to be phased out in the future. This will not be due to the United States surrendering or to the Philippines overcoming the U.S. opposition. It will be more due to defense technology changes (as mentioned above) that makes these bases about as meaningful as the Maginot Line in France in 1940, Pearl Harbor in the United States in 1941, or the Singapore guns pointing to the sea in 1942. The phasing out will also be due to recent world changes that seem to greatly decrease the likelihood of a world war between the Soviet Union, Eastern Europe, and China on the one hand, and the United States and its allies on the other hand.

More important than a natural rather than a forced phase-out is a second key element of a possible super-optimum solution. This element emphasizes massive credits to upgrade the Philippine economy. It could involve no payment of cash whatsoever on the part of the United States and yet provide tremendous economic benefits to the Republic of the Philippines. It involves a number of characteristics. First of all, the United States makes available an amount of credits that when expressed in dollars would be about twice as many dollars as the United States would be willing to pay In the form of rent or a cash payment. The United States would be willing to pay more in the form of credits because:

1. It is normally a lot easier to give credit than to pay cash. An example might be returning merchandise to a store and asking for cash. One may receive various negative reactions as to why the merchandise should be kept. If, however, one asks for a credit slip, the decision-maker is likely to be much more accommodating.
2. The American economy would substantially benefit if the credits could only be used in the United States to buy American products and services. That would benefit the United States more than paying out cash that then gets spent in Japan or elsewhere. At the same time, it does not substantially hamper the Philippines in buying products and services needed for upgrading its economy.
3. The U.S. economy would also substantially benefit indirectly from an upgrading of the Philippine economy, since that would enable the Philippines to buy even more American products and services in the future.

As for what the credits would be for, that is where the Philippines could especially benefit. The shopping list might include such things as:

1. Credits to pay for personnel and facilities for on-the-job training and adult education to upgrade worker productivity.
2. Relevant credits for upgrading Philippine higher education, especially in fields that relate to engineering and public policy which could have high marginal rates of return.

3. Relevant credits for upgrading elementary and secondary education as part of a large-scale investment in human resource development.
4. Relevant credits for seeds, pesticides, herbicides, and farm equipment to make the previously mentioned land reform programs more successful, including the hiring of experts for training programs.
5. Relevant credits for subsidizing suburban job opportunities, regional cities, and overseas employment opportunities.
6. Relevant credits to improve energy and electricity production in the Philippines which is such an important aspect of improving the gross national product.
7. Relevant credits for buying technologies that can improve productivity along with upgraded skills, including modern assembly line technologies.
8. Relevant credits for health care and housing that can be shown to be related to increased worker productivity.
9. Other credits for buying American products and services that relate to upgrading the Philippine economy, as contrasted to buying consumer goods or other products and services that have little increased productivity payoff.

There are additional benefits for both sides that should be mentioned. By both sides in this context is meant the Republic of the Philippines and the United States. Both sides also refers to the liberals and conservatives within the Philippines. Some additional features are:

1. By providing credits rather than cash, there is a minimum of loss due to corruption. It is a lot easier to pocket money than it is to pocket a new schoolhouse or an expert consultant in on-the-job training.
2. By providing credits that are earmarked for upgrading the economy, there is a minimum of loss due to wasteful expenditures including bureaucratic administration.
3. Waste is not going to be completely eliminated. We would not want a straitjacket system that discourages experimentation with innovative ideas for increasing productivity. If innovation is going to be encouraged, some waste must be expected since not all innovative ideas work out well.
4. This could set a precedent for future American aid to other countries and future aid by other developed countries to developing countries. The key aspect of the precedent is emphasizing credits for upgrading the economy, as contrasted to an emphasis on food, shelter, clothing, and other traditional charitable do-gooderism.
5. In that regard, we are talking about teaching people how to fish, rather than giving them a fish. The fishing analogy is endorsed by liberals who founded the Peace Corps and conservatives who believe in workfare rather than charitable handouts. Actually we are talking about teaching people how to develop and apply new technologies for doing such things as fishing, growing crops, manufacturing products, transporting commuters, and making public policy decisions.
6. The kind of program that most wins friends and influences people in favor of the United States might be programs that involve bringing left-wing anti-Americans to the United States to receive training or having American trainers go to work with Philippine union leaders or Mindinao farmers. People acquire a much more favorable attitude toward Americans in that context than by receiving a sack of flour labeled Made in the U.S.A.

It might be noted that if the Filipinos emphasize how obsolete the bases are becoming, they might succeed in getting rid of the bases faster. On the other hand, it might be wise to emphasize how valuable the bases are in order to get even more credits as payment for retaining them. On the third hand, the United States is not so unaware of the empirical realities, and it is not so unaware of bargaining techniques. This idea of retaining the bases along with an inevitable at least partial phase-out and massive credits for upgrading the Philippine economy should not be approached as a matter of traditional negotiation and game playing. Rather it should be approached as a matter that can be resolved to the mutual benefits of all sides in the sense of a super-optimum solution with all major viewpoints coming out ahead of their initial best expectations. Also see Table 22-2 .

Table 22-2. Simplified Table on Phillipine-U.S. Military Bases

Goals **Alternatives**	**CONS** **Conservative concerns**	**LIB** **1. Liberal concerns** **2. Sovereignty**
CONS Bases and more money	+	-
LIB No bases	-	+
NEUTRAL Phase out	0	0
SOS OR WIN-WIN Bases and massive credits to upgrade economy	++	++

II. Two Super Powers

This chapter extends multi-criteria dispute resolution (MCDR) to the international level. It uses as an example the arms control dispute between the United States and the USSR. This chapter, like other illustrative examples in this book, seeks to go beyond the case study aspects to find broader methodological and substantive implications. An appendix to this chapter updates some of this material.

In drafting scholarly articles and probably articles in general, researchers and authors tend to present only the tip of the research, meaning only the portion of the research activities that has been most successful, as measured by various standards. Some of those standards are overly mechanistic, such as measures of statistical significance, rather than policy relevance. This chapter comes closer to being a stream of consciousness regarding the development of a way of viewing the arms control situation from an MCDR perspective.

The chapter proceeds through the following developmental stages:

1. Viewing the alternatives as being accept or reject, but then rejecting those dichotomous alternatives as being unduly confining.
2. Viewing the goals as being to promote the national interest, but then deciding that such a holistic objective function is overly general.
3. Viewing the issues in terms of types of arms inspection and types of arms reduction, but then deciding that a super-optimum solution may need more alternatives, especially a super-optimizing alternative.
4. Thinking about other variations that relate to the development of compromise position, the weighting of goals, the linking of arms control with regional disputes, the possibility of third-party mediation, and other relevant ideas.[1]

III. VIEWING THE NEGOTIATIONS AS AN ACCEPT-REJECT SITUATION

A. The Alternatives

If we were to do an arms control negotiation example for illustrative purposes, the alternatives might be reject the agreement and accept the agreement. These alternatives are analogous to going to trial versus an out-of-court settlement.

1. The Criteria

The criteria would be roughly the same from a U.S. perspective or a Soviet perspective except what would be a benefit to the United States would be a cost to the Soviet Union, and vice versa, if this were being considered as analogous to negotiations over damages for going to trial. Maybe it should not be considered in that light except in a very gross way. The United States is not like a plaintiff seeking damages from the Soviet Union, or vice versa. It is more like negotiating a collective bargaining contract.

As for the U.S.-USSR criteria, they would include intrusive inspection. This is one of the goals of the United States. It may be one of the goals of the Soviet Union too, although less so since they are able to find out what is going on in the United States more easily, given American openness.

Asymmetrical arms reduction is a Soviet goal, but asymmetrical in their favor rather than in the U.S. favor. All this could be worked out better on the computer than on paper so we could see what is happening in terms of scoring, tentative conclusions, and sensitivity analysis. The object is to develop a package to which both sides will want to agree. The

[1] For further details on arms control in general, see Ralph Goldman, *Arms Control and Peace Keeping: Feeling Safe in This World* (New York: Random House, 1982); Alva Myrdal, *The Game of Disarmament: How the United States and Russia Run the Arms Race* (New York: Pantheon, 1982); William Epstein and Bernard Feld, eds., *New Directions in Disarmament* (New York: Praeger, 198 1); and Michael May, George Bing, and John Steinbruner, *Strategic Arms Reductions* (Washington, DC: Brookings Institution, 1988).

package should be of such a nature that settling wins over rejecting given the values of both sides in terms of criteria, weights, and relation scores.

For the sake of simplicity we do not need more than about two goals. On the matter of each of those two goals, Table 22-3, sections A and B, shows both the U.S. and USSR perspectives. They are both concerned with the same alternatives, namely whether to accept or reject an agreement. They are both concerned with the same criteria, namely inspection and mutual reduction. In a broader sense, those are the criteria.

2. The Relations

In terms of giving relation scores, the United States will be much more likely to accept if intrusive inspection is provided. Maybe we need to break the inspection criteria into nonintrusive and intrusive. Likewise we have to break reduction into three parts: asymmetrical favoring the Soviet Union, symmetrical favoring neither side, and asymmetrical favoring the United States. This is shown in Table 22-3C.

B. Possible Combinations on Inspection and Reduction

Maybe a better way to view the situation is not in terms of alternatives that are called "accepting" versus "rejecting" (analogous to settling versus going to trial), but instead to see the alternatives as being what we had been considering the criteria. Thus one could have six possible types of agreements here, and the question is, which should the United States accept of those six possible agreements.

Table 22-3: Viewing the Arms Control Negotiations As An Accept-Reject Situation, Rather than As One Involving Multiple Alternatives

A. Us Perspective

	Inspection	Reduction
Accept		
Reject		

B. U.S.S.R. Perspective

	Inspection	Reduction
Accept		
Reject		

C. Multiple Criteria

	Non-Intrusive Inspection	Intrusive Inspection	Asymmetrical Reduction Favoring USSR	Symmetrical Reduction	Asymmetrical Reduction Favoring USA
Accept					
Reject					

1. No Middle Alternatives and One Criterion

The first alternative is nonintrusive favoring the USSR, the second nonintrusive symmetrical, the third nonintrusive favoring the U.S., the fourth intrusive favoring the USSR, the fifth intrusive symmetrical, and the sixth intrusive favoring the United States. These could be rank ordered, which might provide some useful insights. And likewise, the alternatives can be rank ordered from the Soviet perspective. This seems like it is leading to a traditional compromise, though, and not a super-optimum solution.

If the six alternatives are rank ordered from the *U.S. perspective*, then clearly the one that would get the highest score of the six would be intrusive and favoring the United States. The one that would get the lowest score would be nonintrusive and favoring the USSR. Presumably, which side gets favored is more important than whether the inspection is nonintrusive or intrusive. Thus the fifth best alternative would be number 3. The second from the bottom would be number 4. With the six rank ordered, one could then assume that the USSR national interest would result in the opposite rank order for those same six alternatives.

If the numbers are reversed to get the *USSR perspective*, then the 6 and the 1 change places. The 5 and the 2 should change places as well. That doesn't seem right. Each rank has to be thought out separately instead of just using a mechanical formula to convert the U.S. ranks into the Soviet ranks. The Soviets presumably are more concerned with whom the reduction favors than whether the inspection is intrusive or not. Thus they would consider alternative 4 as being the second best and the next to the bottom alternative as being nonintrusive favoring the United States. If one looks at the results, the 6 and the 1 have been switched around, so have the 5 and the 2, and so have the 3 and the 4 (see Table 22-6).

2. Middling Alternatives and Multiple Criteria

This clearly leads to a compromise position. If the United States and the USSR have equal voting power as to which alternative will be accepted, then the total scores would be a tie of 7 for all the alternatives. The compromise position would be a middle alternative. The middle alternative, though, on a 1-6 scale is either a 4 or a 3. A 4 is intrusive favoring the USSR, 3 is nonintrusive favoring the United States. That is splitting the difference on a combined criterion . It makes more sense to talk in terms of splitting the difference on each criterion separately, which gets into a more meaningful kind of multi-criteria analysis. Table 22-4 in effect provides a single objective function for each side and distorts the results. Table 22-5 emphasizes that there are two criteria operating: inspection and reduction.

Looking at the multi-criteria perspective of Table 22-5, the measurement scale on inspection looks like a 1 to 2 scale, unless we provide for some kind of middle that is neither nonintrusive nor intrusive. That would make for nine alternatives. That does make more sense, not just because it makes the multi-dimensionality problem easier, but because it is a false dichotomy to talk about nonintrusive and intrusive. Purely nonintrusive would mean that the only inspection would come from satellites. the most intrusive inspection would be satellites plus permanently stationed ground observers. The middling position would be satellites plus intrusive inspectors who don't permanently live at the locations but who make periodic inspections once a week, once a month, or whatever is agreed to. If the middling position is taken, then one would have to get into the issue of how often the inspections would occur. One might also have to get into further details as to exactly what gets inspected, considering nine alternatives arranged in somewhat random order.

Table 22-4. Possible Combinations on Inspection and Reduction Without Allowing for Middling Positions

A. U.S. Perspective

	USA National Interest
1. N–USSR	1
2. N–S	3
3. N–USA	5
4. I–USSR	2
5. I–S	4
6. I–USA	6

B. USSR Perspective

	USSR National Interest	**Total Score**
1. N–USSR	6	7 = 1 +6
2. N–S	4	7 = 3 + 4
3. N–USA	2	7 = 5 + 2
4. I–USSR	5	7 = 2 + 5
5. I–S	3	7 = 4 +3
6. I–USA	1	7 = 6 +1

Notes:

1. Intrusiveness of inspection as an alternative: N = Non-intrusive; I = Intrusive
2. Who is favored on arms reduction: USSR = Favoring USSR on arms reduction; USA = Favoring USA on arms reduction; S = Symmetrical
3. The numbers under USA and USSR national interest are rank orders from 1 to 6 for the six alternatives

Table 22-5A shows the data file considering inspection to be on a 1:3 scale and reduction to be on a 1:3 scale. For the moment both inspection and reduction are given equal weight, although reduction is likely to be more important. Nonintrusive gets a score of 1, between a score of 2, and intrusive a score of 3. On the matter of reduction, favoring the USSR gets a score of 1, symmetrical a score of 2, and favoring USA a score of 3. Thus from the U.S. perspective if these two goals are weighted equally, the clear winner is intrusive inspection favoring the United States. We also now have a way of scoring all nine alternatives.

On Table 22-5B we look at the same set of nine alternatives from the Soviet Union's perspective. They are also concerned with the goals of inspection and reduction, measured on a 1:3 scale. The difference is that they perceive the relation scores for each alternative and each goal differently than the United States does, so that nonintrusive gets a score of 3, between a score of 2, and intrusive a score of 1. Likewise, favoring the USSR gets a score of 3, symmetrical a score of 2, and favoring the United States a score of 1. The total scores thus wind up in the opposite direction. If we add these total scores together we probably come up with a perfect tie of 8 for every alternative.

Table 22-5. Possible Combinations on Inspection and Reduction

A. US Perspective

	Inspection W = 1	Reduction W = 2 Unweighted	Reduction W = 2 Weighted	Totals Unweighted	Totals Weighted
1. N–USSR	1	1	2	2	3
2. N–S	1	2	4	3	5
3. N–USA	1	3	6	4	7
4. B–USSR	2	1	2	3	4
5. B–S	2	2	4	4	6
6. B–USA	2	3	6	5	8
7. I–USSR	3	1	2	4	5
8. I–S	3	2	4	5	7
9. I–USA	3	3	6	6	9

B. USSR Perspective

	Inspection W = 1	Reduction W = 2 Unweighted	Reduction W = 2 Weighted	Totals Unweighted	Totals Weighted	US-USSR Sum
1. N–USSR	3	3	6	6	9	8 = 2+6
2. N–S	3	2	4	5	7	8 = 3+5
3. N–USA	3	1	2	4	5	8 = 4+4
4. B–USSR	2	3	6	5	8	8 = 3+5
5. B–S	2	2	4	4	6	8 = 4+4
6. D–USA	2	1	2	3	4	8 = 5+3
7. I–USSR	1	3	6	4	7	8 = 4+4
8. I–S	1	2	4	3	5	8 = 5+3
9. I–USA	1	1	2	2	3	8 = 6+2

Notes:

1. B = Both non-intrusive and intrusive, meaning partly non-intrusive and partly intrusive
2. The 1-3 scale under inspection refers to rank orders from 1 to 3 on the three inspection alternatives
3. Likewise, the 1-3 scale under reduction refers to rank orders from 1 to 3 on the tree reduction alternatives in the unweighted column.
4. The weighted column under reduction is the unweighted column multiplied by a weight of 2.
5. The unweighted totals involve adding the inspection column and the unweighted reduction column.
6. The weighted totals involve adding the inspection column and the weighted reduction column.
7. The US-USSR sum involves adding the unweighted US total and the unweighted USSR total.

Table 22-6 shows the logical *compromise*, which is not what we are looking for but is worth pointing out. The logical compromise is to go to the "between category on inspection and the "symmetrical" category on reduction. That could be shown in Table 22-6 as a compromiser's perspective. The compromise is faced with the same nine alternatives and the same two goals or criteria of inspection and reduction. The big difference is that the compromiser scores each category differently than either the USSR or the United States would. For the compromiser there may really only be a 1:2 scale. A 1:3 scale makes sense: 3 means conducive to a compromise, 1 means negative to a compromise, and 2 means neutral. Either nonintrusive or intrusive is contrary to a compromise. Between is in conformity. Likewise on reduction, either favoring the USSR or the United States is adverse to a compromise. Taking the in-between position is favorable, meaning it gets a 3. Thus from the compromiser's perspective, alternative number 5 is clearly the winner and the worst alternatives are nonintrusive favoring one side or the other or intrusive favoring one side or the other. In between are nonintrusive or intrusive but symmetrical or the middling position on inspection but favoring the USSR or the USA.

Table 22-6. Possible Combinations on Inspection and Reduction from a Mediator's Perspective

Compromise Perspective	Inspection W =1	Reduction W = 2 Unweighted	Weighted	Totals Unweighted	Weighted
1. N–USSR	1	1	2	2	3
2. N–S	1	3	6	4	7
3. N–USA	1	1	2	2	3
4. B–USSR	3	1	2	4	5
5. B–S	3	3	6	6	9
6. B–USA	3	1	2	4	5
7. I–USSR	1	1	2	2	3
8. I–S	1	3	6	4	4
9. I–USA	1	1	2	2	3

Notes:

1. The leters in Table 22-6 have the same meaning as those in 22-4 and 22-5.
2. The numbers in Table 22-6 have the same meaning as those in 22-5.

C. Weighting the Goals

If we bring in weights then we get slightly different results, not so much regarding which alternative wins, but with regard to the scores of all the alternatives. The weighted scores on reduction can be shown in a separate column, giving reduction twice the weight of inspection.

First looking at how that affects the U.S. perspective, alternative number 9 still comes out the clear winner, but there are more distinctions and less ties. There are only two ties, namely alternatives 2 and 7 look equally bad from the *U.S. perspective*. We could break those ties by giving even more weight to reduction. It is not especially important, though. It could be for mediation purposes, what the exact scores are below first place. That definitely is important since this is mediated decision-making. It would not be at all important if the United States were making a decision all by itself or the USSR were making a decision all by itself. Although even'then one might want to know what it takes to bring a second-place alternative up to first place, or some other alternative up to first place. And then it might be important to know more precisely how far out of first place the other place alternative is, or what the size of the gap is.

Look at how the weights affect the *USSR perspective*. It results in producing the exact set of weights except in reverse order, because we may have an unrealistic symmetry of weights. Just because the United States places twice as much weight on reduction as on inspection does not mean the Soviet Union does too. The Soviet Union may not feel as strongly about inspection as the United States does, meaning that there is a big gap, or a bigger gap between the weights. If the Soviet Union is primarily concerned with reduction and does not care much about inspection, then maybe reduction is at least three times as important for the Soviet Union, whereas it is only twice as important for the United States.

Look at the weights from the *compromise perspective*. The winner even more strongly is now number 5. The loser likewise even more strongly in the sense of the gap is still numbers I and 9, which are at the extremes. The way we laid this out, though, is not a bell-shaped curve because 7 is just as extreme as 9, and 3 is just as extreme as 1. In second place is nonintrusive inspection with symmetrical reduction. The reason for this is because symmetrical reduction is very important from a compromiser's perspective and may he easier to achieve than any kind of intrusive inspection. The reason for its importance, though, is not that it is easier to achieve, but because it is given high weight by both the United States and the USSR. Thus it is more important to compromise on reduction since it is more emotionally dividing the two disputants than inspection is (see Table 22-6).

IV. Bringing in Regional Issues

We could expand to include more criteria besides inspection and reduction, such as bringing in regional conflicts. The nuclear-free zone idea is no longer seriously discussed, nor is the testing idea because it has been achieved. In the case of the nuclear-free zone it has not been achieved but seems unlikely to be achieved. It would mean withdrawal of all missiles whatsoever from most of Eastern and Western Europe, or all nuclear missiles. One could argue that to a considerable extent that has happened already as a result of arms control agreements, although it is not referred to as a nuclear-free zone. It is referred to as the Intermediate-Range Nuclear Forces arms control treaty. There would be no reason for having long-range missiles in Europe since they would have to travel only a relatively short distance to get to the Soviet Union. It is not a nuclearfree zone because there are short-range missiles still tolerated. There is nothing in the treaty that says West Germany cannot have nuclear tipped artillery that are capable of being fired only a short distance.

An expert systems approach on this would probably have to work with a spreadsheet unless it just involves some very general clich6s like saying to obtain an agreement one needs to compromise and not just push for what favors one side or the other. Those kinds of expert systems principles are not much help in arriving at specific agreements in arms control or anyplace else.

As for the super-optimum solution, it does require possibly adding some additional criteria in order to have the United States make concessions on some things that are not so important to it but important to the Soviet Union, and vice versa. This is where the regional agreements could come in.

A. Afghanistan

Afghanistan would be one of the regional agreements. Afghanistan really is not so important to the United States. It is on the other side of the world. There are not many Afghan voters in the United States who are going to be upset about the U.S. position on Afghanistan. Afghanistan is important to the Soviet Union. It is on its southern border. The Soviet Union has lost a lot of lives in Afghanistan. The United States could make what appears to be a big concession of agreeing not to arm the Afghan rebels further in return for the Soviet Union withdrawing. That is something that would be important to the Soviet Union. They could withdraw without losing face with their people still in power and maybe likely to remain there if the United States does not arm the Afghan rebels. The rebels have no way of overthrowing the government without American arms. Without those arms they would be fighting with sticks, stones, and some old World War I rifles. One could go through all the regional conflicts and work out a similar kind of arms control agreement.

B. Nicaragua

Nicaragua is very emotionally important to the United States. The Soviet Union would be willing to stop arming the Sandinistas just as the United States would be willing to stop arming the Afghan rebels. The result in both places would not be a government change at all, but with everybody saving face. The Contras have no more chance of overthrowing the Sandinistas without American arms than the Afghan rebels have. By the Soviet Union withdrawing, it is not causing the Sandinista regime to collapse, but it could be looked upon as a victory for the United States just as the Cubans withdrawing from Angola can be.

One irony of all this is that the liberals have traditionally opposed bringing regional conflicts into an arms control agreement on grounds that it messes up the arms control agreement to bring in side issues. On the contrary, it is easier to get an arms control agreement because it is the side issues where each side can make concessions that are important to the other side but not important to it. They cannot do that so well on the pure arms control issues. The Soviet Union is not going to make a concession saying that they will agree to an asymmetrical reduction in which they do more reducing than the United States does. Likewise the United States is not going to make a concession saying that it will reduce more than the Soviet Union does. On the matter of inspection, the United States legitimately needs to have intrusive inspection in order to make sure the agreement is complied with. It is not a sneaky way of doing spying that is unrelated to the arms control agreement. The Soviet Union, on the other hand, does not need intrusive inspection as much. Actually, neither side needs much intrusive inspection, given the power of satellite surveillance. To a considerable extent the issue is a symbolic one. It is a leftover from presatellite days. It goes back to arms control agreements that never were agreed to back in the later 1940s and early 1950s. It can easily be handled through old fashioned compromise rather than super-optimum solution by just agreeing to some middling position. The regional conflicts are necessary to having a super-optimum solution.

C. Angola

Maybe Angola would also include Mozambique and Namibia. Maybe not Mozambique since the U.S. does not support the anticommunist group there. Nobody supports them, at least no government does. Maybe it also would not have to include Namibia since the U.S. pays lip service to the rebels there. In other words, it does not have to include any part of the world where conflict is going on unless the United States is on one side and the Soviet Union on the other side as in Afghanistan, Nicaragua, and Angola.

D. Other Competitive Places

The United States and Soviet Union are on opposite sides in almost every country in the world, but where there is no armed conflict going on, there is nothing that could be very easily compromised or mediated. The Soviet Union is not going to agree to stop supporting the French Communist party if the United States will agree to stop supporting the French Right Wing parties. That kind of competition should be encouraged, not discouraged. It is fine for the USSR and the United States to be trying to convince through nonviolent means that its form of government is best. It is logical to work through friendly political parties in other countries to do that kind of convincing. There should be no agreements that they will hold back on trying to win friends and influence people. That probably should include Radio Free Europe and Voice of America, too. From the point of view of world free speech, it is undesirable for the Soviet Union to ask the United States to stop sending broadcasts to the Soviet Union or for the United States to agree to stop doing so, especially if it is a private-enterprise activity like Radio Free Europe, or even if it is a government agency Re the Voice of America. One could argue that it would he legitimate for the United States to agree to hold back on lying and distortion of the truth but not on reasonably objective presentations. The lying and distortion seem to have decreased greatly in recent years, partly because they have been so unsuccessful.

E. Other Violent Places

As for other places where violence is occurring, where the United States is arming one side and the Soviet Union is arming the other side, we should talk in terms of regions not specific countries. Thus Nicaragua includes El Salvador in that context. There is some question as to whether it includes Guatemala and Peru. There is a fine line between guerrilla warfare, especially urban guerrilla warfare and political party action and economic action that includes strikes that sometimes involve sit-down activity and physical confrontations between the strikers and police. If a communist-led union in Bolivia in the mines goes on strike and the army starts shooting, that is very different than Afghanistan, Angola, and Nicaragua. The

Soviet Union could even legitimately say that it does not have complete control over every communist group in the world. Many of them are native groups who receive no particular help from the Soviet Union. The Bolivian miners are an example, They have been strongly communist since before the Soviet Union came to Latin America.

One cannot get too formal about these definitions, though. One does not expect rebels in El Salvador or elsewhere who are seeking to overthrow a right-wing government to wear uniforms as if they were a regular army. It just so happens that when the U.S. arms rebels to overthrow a communist government like the Sandinistas or the Angolan government, one of the things we especially do is to provide them with uniforms. This may do more harm than good. It probably interferes with their looking like the people with whom they are supposed to become meshed. It causes them to look like some kind of foreign invading army. The State Department and CIA do it in order to make the right-wing rebels look better organized. It probably hurts their effectiveness. The communists seem to do pretty well fighting in whatever kind of pajamas they can find in Vietnam, without fancy brimmed hats.

F. Increasing the Matrix

The overall conclusion here is that we will do a data file that will consist of five goals: inspection, reduction, Afghanistan, Nicaragua, and Angola. The quantity of agreements becomes 3 times 3 times 2 times 2 times 2 or 72 agreements. We probably do not need all 72 since some are obviously too extreme in favor of one side or the other. For a starter, though, we can think in terms of all 72. It means about five data files at 15 each, which adds up to 75 alternatives. It would be a good example of multiple alternatives. We would immediately eliminate all the alternatives that wind up with total scores from the U.S. perspective that are higher than a certain cutoff or with total scores from the USSR perspective that are higher than a certain cutoff, since there is virtually no chance those agreements would be reached. We would work with two separate data files (maybe three) using the compromiser's perspective too.

V. Broader Goals and Alternatives

A. National Security and Income as Goals

In talking about the goals that are involved in the arms control negotiation, we have emphasized the more intermediate goals that relate to inspection and reduction and possibly Afghanistan, Angola, and Nicaragua. We could talk in terms. of higher goals that relate to national security and the GNP. It is relatively easy to do here, possibly because the intermediate goals are so closely associated with the alternatives that we are really not talking about three different levels, but instead we are talking about five or six issues that are like budget categories. The budget categories are not the alternatives. The alternatives are how much to allocate to each budget category. This allows for a tremendous quantity of alternatives.

Likewise, the five issues allow for about 72 alternatives. The problem could be viewed the way it is shown in Table 22-7 as involving five semialternatives of inspection, reduction, Afghanistan, Angola, and Nicaragua, from the U.S. perspective and the Soviet perspective. The goals are national security and GNP. Looking first at the U.S. perspective, scoring these on a 1-5 scale, inspection is irrelevant to the GNP. It is about 3.5 on national security. It is not higher on national security because it is a symmetrical reduction, meaning that the United States and the Soviet Union are still equally powerful, although both less powerful than they formerly were.

Table 22-7. Trade as a Dominating Alternative Among the Arms Control and Regional Issues

A. USA Perspective

	National Security	GNP	Totals	Ranks
Semi-Inspection	4.5	3	7.5	3
Mutual Reduction	3.5	5	8.5	1
Settle Afghanistan	3.5	3.5	7	4
Settle Nicaragua	4	4	8	2
Trade	4	5	9	>1

B. USSR perspective

	National Security	GNP	Totals	Ranks
Semi-Inspection	3	3	6	4
Mutual Reduction	3.5	5	8.5	1
Settle Afghanistan	4	4	8	2
Settle Nicaragua	3+	3.5	6.5+	3
Trade	4	5	9	>1

Notes:

1. The numbers in the national security column and the GNP column are relation scores on a 1-5 scale. A 5 means that the alternative is highly conducive to the goal; a 4 means mildy conducive; a 3 means neither conducive nor adverse; a 2 means mildy adverse; and a 1 means highly adverse.
2. The numbers in the totals column involve summing the numbers in the national security and GNP columns.
3. The numbers in the ranks show rank orders from 1 to 4 for the four alternatives other than international trade. International trade does better than the alternative that was previously ranked first.

B. Regional Issues as More Alternatives

Let us continue the analysis of the arms control situation from the perspective of issues on the rows rather than alternatives and goals on the columns. Afghanistan is irrelevant to the U.S. GNP and largely irrelevant to our national security. Angola is slightly more relevant to national security, given some strategic minerals, but not especially relevant to the GNP. We should recognize that there is a substantial amount of money being spent even if it is not a huge amount. One drawback to talking about issues rather than alternatives is that the issue itself is not so important to national security or GNP. It is what is done on the issue. Therefore, we have to assume a kind of middling position is aely to result on the issue. In that sense, settling Afghanistan would be slightly more helpful to the U.S. GNP than not settling Afghanistan. Give it a 3.5. Settling Angola is just a + 3 since it is costing the United States less money. Settling Nicaragua is at least a 4 since that is a big investment.

On the national security side, settling Nicaragua is a 4. Settling Afghanistan could be considered a 3.5 just like the GNP effect because an explosive Afghanistan could be more likely to directly involve the U.S., more so than Angola. If the Afghanistan war spreads to Pakistan then the United States is much more likely to be involved given our treaty obligations to Pakistan. If the Angola war spreads to Zaire, Zambia, or other surrounding countries, it does not especially involve the United States. Thus, where the United States is spending the most money is where U.S. national security is perceived as being most threatened. Therefore on those three regional conflicts, the GNP score and the national security score are about the same.

C. Inspection and Reduction

The important thing to note is that mutual reduction is more important than inspection with regard to GNP, although inspection may be more important to national security. This 1-5 scale does not bring out differences sufficiently, though, because a 5 is the highest score that can be given to the effect of mutual reduction on GNP. If settling Nicaragua is a 4 on the 1-5 scale, then mutual reduction would be about a 50 on a 1-5 scale, but there is no provision for anything above 5. This illustrates the need for working with a 0- 100 scale. Then we could easily show that settling Nicaragua would have an effect on the U.S. GNP of about 60 on a 0-100 scale, but a mutual arms reduction would have an effect of about 95. The difference between 60 and 95 on a 0-100 scale is much more than the difference between 4 and 5 on a 1-5 scale.

If we add across using this approach we do not get anything meaningful. All we get is that mutual reduction is the most important issue, followed by Nicaragua and then inspection and then Afghanistan and then Angola. This could be useful for arriving at weights concerning the relative importance of those issues or intermediate goals. It does not seem to be especially useful in seeing anything with regard to what would be a super-optimum solution, although in order to get insights into that it is necessary to see the Soviet perspective.

D. The Soviet Perspective

The Soviet perspective with the same five issues and the same two goals will result in a different rank order on the importance of these issues that could lend itself to seeing that the United States could make some concessions on matters that are not so important to it but are relatively more important to the Soviet Union, and vice versa, although that could come out from the previous analysis.

We never did carry out the previous analysis to include the regional conflicts of the matter of GNP. The Soviet Union would give a 5 to reduction and maybe also only a 3 to inspection since inspection does not cost as much money, regardless which category is chosen. They would give a 4 to settling Afghanistan, probably a 3.5 to settling Nicaragua, and just a + 3 on Angola. They are putting the most money in Afghanistan, the least in Angola, with Nicaragua in the middle. The United States is putting the most in Nicaragua, the least in Angola, and Afghanistan in the middle. On national security, they would give about a 3.5 on mutual reduction. They might consider inspection as a - 3 since they feel it jeopardizes their national security to allow inspection of their weapons systems. Settling Afghanistan might be worth about a 4 in terms of their national security since it is draining military resources and lowering military morale. Angola is about a + 3. Nicaragua is about a + 3 too. If Nicaragua were to fall to the Contras this would not jeopardize the Soviet national security. And if it were to stay in the hands of the Sandinistas it would not greatly help the Soviet security. It gets a 3 + though, because settling any regional conflict decreases the possibility of an unwanted war occurring between the Soviet Union and the United States.

If we add across we can see that the rank order is different for the Soviet Union as to how important settling these matters are. The most important is getting an arms reduction because of the value to the GNP. Next in importance is settling the Afghanistan matter. And then comes Nicaragua and inspection, with Angola being last on both lists and reduction being first. The order in between on numbers 2, 3, and 4 are a bit different. The United States considers Nicaragua highly important. The Soviet Union considers Afghanistan highly important. After that it is about a toss-up from the U.S. perspective as to the importance of inspection versus Afghanistan, with inspection maybe slightly more important. On the Soviet Union side, after second-place Afghanistan it is a toss-up between inspection and Nicaragua, with Nicaragua maybe being slightly more important because it is more expensive, but inspection is more important on national security.

E. Mutually Beneficial Compromise

With this kind of information it is logical for the United States to make concessions on Afghanistan since it is relatively unimportant to the United States and highly important to the Soviet Union. Likewise, it makes sense for the Soviet Union to make concessions on Nicaragua since Nicaragua is not so important to the Soviet Union but is much more important to the United States. It would simplify things to leave Angola out of this analysis since it is not very important to either side. It does not have that much national security significance or GNP significance. We then work with four issues. We could mention other regional conflicts and other arms control issues without explicitly including them.

This kind of situation lends itself well to a mediator since both sides want a reduction, at least a mutual reduction, because it will be good for their GNPs while at the same time not jeopardizing their national security if the reduction leaves both sides in the same position as they were before in terms of who is more powerful militarily. It is a good situation for a mediator because even though both sides want virtually the same thing, there are emotional involvements that prevent them from coming up with alternatives that will save face and not look like each side is surrendering. There is no mediator, though, in the arms control negotiations partly because it is kind of a loss of face even to have a mediator, let alone to agree to anything a mediator suggests. Mediators are for lesser powers. When the two superpowers of the world negotiate, the idea of a mediator seems out of place if the mediator is supposed to be someone who has higher authority than either of the disputants.

F. Adding International Trade as an SOS Alternative

We could add some global policy problem issues even if they are not part of the negotiations. We have added Afghanistan and Nicaragua, which are not really part of the negotiations. An additional issue that would make sense is international trade, which mainly means that the United States gives farm products and manufactured products in return for whatever cash the Soviet Union can come up with plus natural resource products such as oil if the Soviet Union were willing to part with some of its oil. It is the world's second largest oil producer, but uses all its oil domestically and exports almost nothing. It could export to the United States, an oil-buying country, even though it may still be a large oil producer but its oil needs are greater than it can satisfy. The Soviet Union would then have to buy oil elsewhere, but as part of a multilateral trading might be able to offer products that people elsewhere would like to have but the United States is not especially interested in. In that regard, about 20% of the Soviet people are Moslems, who manufacture products that could be of interest to Arab countries who would sell oil to Russia in return for Moslem-related products. The Soviet Union would then be able to satisfy its oil needs while at the same time selling oil to the United States in return for farm products and manufactured goods.

One general point is that trading in goods holds out great possibilities for super-optimum solutions because the selling side tends to have a surplus of whatever it is selling and would rather have whatever it is getting than what it is getting rid of, and likewise with the buying side. In the context, both sides are buying and selling. More specifically, this kind of trade deal of food and manufactured goods for raw materials could include iron ore and lots of minerals. The Soviet Union is the world's leading gold producer and it may be the leading mineral producer in almost every field of minerals. It should be exporting a lot more raw materials, which would do wonders for its GNP. It could even help national security by lowering tensions, and anything that increases its economy also increases national security. Likewise with the United States, meaning a score of 5 on GNP for trade and a score of 4 for national security. It makes trade a 9 on both sides.

This makes trade the super-optimum alternative. These are not mutually exclusive alternatives, though they are issues, all of which can play a part in an agreement. The key thing is that trade becomes even more important than arms reduction, although that is partly because we are operating only on a 1-5 scale and both arms reduction and trade get the maximum possible on GNP when in reality arms reduction should be even higher than a 5. If we were to do this over again we would possibly use a 0- 100 scale. The important thing in this situation is not whether trade is more important than arms reduction-this is not a mutually exclusive situation where only one best alternative wins-it is that the combination of arms reduction and trade is so much better than arms reduction alone.

VI. SOME IMPLICATIONS

One thing this also illustrates is that if big thinking is going to occur in these international negotiations, the negotiators need to be broader-minded people than the usual State Department diplomacy people who only know negotiations that have to do with military matters and peace treaties, who do not know about trade. Trade is the realm of the Department of Commerce, which for that matter does not really know much about regional politics, and maybe not even much about military matters since that is for the Department of Defense. The regional politics issues require area specialists who supposedly do exist in the State Department, but they are area specialists on the military aspects of Afghanistan and Nicaragua and not the total political, social, economic aspects. The place to find people like that is outside the government, maybe among academic area specialists.

It is conceivable that someone who is a broad-minded interpersonal generalist could handle this kind of negotiation if he were given the authority to do so. Examples of individuals who are not career government people who have done well in such negotiating roles since World War 11 include Bernard Baruch, Lloyd Cutler, and Max Kampleman. The first was a financier; the other two were lawyers. All three worked for both Democratic and Republican presidents. Kampleman was especially involved in the Reagan arms control negotiations, but he may not have been given the authority to go beyond a discussion of issues of arms reduction and inspection, as contrasted to Afghanistan, Nicaragua, or trade relations. This is an unfortunate missed opportunity to do something that not only does three or four birds with one stone, but enables the original bird to get done better. This is an example where it can be easier to do four things at once than only one thing, because the other three help the one thing to get done.

Thus in the context of super-optimum dispute resolution, doing more can be easier than doing less. Multi-criteria decision-making can be easier in the sense of arriving at better and possibly faster solutions than decision-making that involves a single objective function. Five criteria may be easier to work with than one criterion by allowing for more options. This is especially so in a dispute resolution context, although it may be so in the context of individual decisionmaking, at least with regard to arriving at better solutions, if not faster ones .[2]

---

[2] For further details on international negotiation and mediation, see Roger Fisher, *International Mediation: A Guidefor Practitioners* (Cambridge, MA: Harvard Negotiation Project, 1980); Marie Dugan, ed., *Conflict Resolution*, special issue of Peace and Change, Summer 1982; American Law Institute, *Remedies for Violations of International Law* (Philadelphia: ALI, 1984); and back issues of the *Journal of Conflict Resolution.*

VII. Appendix: A Super-Optimum Perspective on the U.S.-USSR Arms Control Negotiations as of 1990

The purpose of this appendix is to update the chapter in two ways. The first is a substantive way that relates to the fact that since about 1988 the formerly radical idea of arms reduction has become much more accepted, as contrasted to less ambitious alternatives of slowing or freezing the arms race. The second updating involves a clarification of the tabular perspective of presenting or analyzing super-optimum solutions.

Table 22-8 shows how the U.S.-USSR arms control negotiations might be viewed as of 1990. Eight alternative positions are shown-four of the United States and four of the USSR. Each side is faced with basically the same four alternatives,

1. Keep the arms situation as it is. This is the most conservative reasonable alternative as of 1990. It is no longer being actively proposed that the arms race should be increased.
2. Have a big reduction in arms. This is the new liberal alternative. It is interesting to note that liberals were formerly advocating a freeze, which is now in effect the conservative alternative. This is a good example of how yesterday's liberal sometimes becomes today's conservative.
3. Have a little reduction between keeping things as they are and a big reduction. This is logicafly the neutral or compromise position. It typically involves no innovative ideas, but merely splitting the difference between the conservative and liberal positions.
4. Have a super-optimum solution that could consist of a combination of a big reduction and various international trade agreements between the United States and the Soviet Union, or even more broadly between the United States plus Western Europe and the Soviet Union plus Eastern Europe.
5. The four alternatives the Soviet Union is considering are virtually identical. It is often the case in bilateral dispute resolution that both sides are faced with the same alternatives. They differ mainly regarding what their goals are.

Inspection is no longer such a big issue as a result of increased openness on the part of the Soviet Union and improved surveillance technology. Afghanistan is no longer such a controversy in view of the Soviet withdrawal. Likewise, the United States has stopped giving military aid to the Nicaraguan rebels, and it looks as if there will be a reasonably meaningful electoral process in both Nicaragua and Afghanistan.

Table 22-8. A Super-Optimizing Perspective on U.S.-U.S.S.R. Negotiations as of 1990

A. USA Perspective

	National Security (C)	GNP (L)	Neutral Totals	Liberal Totals	Conservative Totals
(C) As is	3	3	12	12	12*
(L) Big Reductions	2	4	12	14*	10
(N) Little Reductions	2.5	3.5	12	13	11
(S) Big Reductions & Trade	4	5	18	19**	17**

B. USSR Perspective

	National Security (C)	GNP (L)	Neutral Totals	Liberal Totals	Conservative Totals
(C) As is	3	3	12	12	12*
(L) Big Reductions	2	4	12	14*	10
(N) Little Reductions	2.5	3.5	12	13	11
(S) Big Reductions & Trade	4	5	18	19**	17**

Notes:

1. The symbols for the alternatives stand for relatively conservative (C), liberal W, nPutral (N), and super-optimum solution (S).
2. The conservative totals involve giving national security a multiplier weight of 3 and GNP a weight of 1. The liberal totals involve giving GNP a weight of 3 and national security a weight of 1. The neutral totals involve giving both national security and GNP a middling weight of 2.
3. The conservative alternative wins on the conservative total before considering the SOS. Likewise the liberal alternative wins on the liberal total, and the neutral alternative on the neutral total.
4. The SOS alternative wins big on all three alternatives for both the USA and the USSR.

On the matter of goals, there are basically only two, although they could be subdivided, and other lesser goals could be added. Since there are two goals on the part of the United States and two on the part of the Soviet Union, there are four goals altogether:

1. Promoting the national security of the United States. This is a relatively conservative goal. It is also endorsed by liberals, especially if the external threat is from a rightwing source, as in World War 11, or even a dictorial left-wing source, as during much of the cold war.
2. Promoting the gross national product of the United States, including the idea of full employment and increased international competitiveness. This is a relatively liberal goal, especially if full employment is emphasized, but also strongly endorsed by

conservatives, especially if the emphasis is on international competitiveness and reduced inflation.

3 Promoting the national security of the Soviet Union. This is definitely an important goal of the Soviet military and also the civilian government. Too often the U.S. State Department takes the position that the Soviet Union has nothing to worry about from the United States. The more important position is not whether they have anything to worry about, but whether they perceive that they have something to worry about.

3. Promoting the gross national product of the Soviet Union, This is also definitely an important goal of the Soviet Union, especially the civilian government and the civilian population. Too often the CIA and people in the State Department take the position that the Soviet Union does not care about consumer goods and raising living standards. It is obvious at least since 1988 (if not before) that people in the Soviet Union and Eastern Europe do want a better quality of life in terms of both economic goods and political accountability.

Table 22-8 shows how U.S. negotiators are likely to perceive the relations between each alternative and each goal. The relations are expressed on a 1-5 scale. A 5 means that if the alternative increases, the goal is likely to increase greatly; a 4 means the goal is likely to increase slightly; a 3 means the goal is not likely to increase or decrease; a 2 means the goal is likely to decrease slightly; and a I means that if the alternative increases, the goal is likely to decrease greatly. If the first alternative is to keep things as they are, that is likely to have no change on either national security or the gross national product. Therefore, a 3 is inserted into the two cells in the top row for both the United States and the USSR. If the second alternative is to have a big reduction in arms, that is likely to be perceived as causing at least a slight decrease in national security by the United States and the USSR. The funds that might be released from such a reduction, however, are likely to be perceived as being capable of increasing the GNPs of both the United States and the USSR by using those funds to develop and diffuse new technologies that will increase each country's economic capabilities.

The third alternative of a small reduction scores a 2.5 on national security between the 3 of doing nothing and the 2 of a big arms reduction. Likewise, a small reduction scores 3.5 on GNP between the 3 of doing nothing and the 4 of a big arms reduction. Like a typical compromise, it achieves the worst and the best of both of the other alternatives. As a result, it generates about the same total score. All three of the traditional alternatives generate total scores of 6 for both the United States and the Soviet Union. That means they are all about equally undesirable or equally desirable. The compromise alternative, however, is more likely to be adopted because it scores higher on the unshown goal of political feasibility. It is more politically feasible because both conservatives and liberals will vote for it as a second choice. They will then console themselves by saying that things could have been worse if the other side had won.

Under a super-optimum solution, both sides do win, and they can win even better than their initial best expectations. At first glance, one might question how can a big reduction plus trade result in more national security than a big reduction alone. This implies that national security is only dependent on how well armed each country is. A country that has a lower GNP than it could have may be weakening itself regarding arms capability and the ability to fight a war. More important, trade between two countries who might otherwise be hostile can create a mutually beneficial interdependence that decreases the likelihood of hostile interaction. Good examples include the unwillingness of the Reagan administration to punish the Soviet Union for its invasion of Afghanistan by prohibiting grain shipments, or the unwillingness of the Bush administration to punish China for its suppression of the pro-democracy movement by invoking trade sanctions. In both cases, the supposedly less anticommunist liberals were more likely to favor the grain embargo and trade sanctions partly because they are less sensitive to the value of international business transactions. In other words, active trading between the United States and the Soviet Union can do more to decrease the likelihood of their going to war and thus to increase their national security than either an arms increase or an arms decrease. This explains the 4 in the SOS row of the national security column.

The 5 in the SOS row of the GNP column reflects the fact that a big reduction alone generates a relation score of a 4 by virtue of the funds that are released from arms development to be available for supply-side economics, industrial policy, and the development of new technologies. It is no coincidence that among the top industrialized countries of the world, Japan and West Germany now score the highest in productivity increases and the lowest in arms expenditures per capita, while they score the lowest in recent productivity increases. In addition to the effect on GNP of the big arms reduction, the SOS also produces a positive effect by virtue of the trade agreements between the West and the East. One might say that the United States does not need the Soviet Union as a trading partner. For that matter, one could say that the United States could survive with no outside trading partners, and maybe the Soviet Union could too. If both countries want to improve their living standards substantially, however, they should take advantage of their potential abilities to buy and sell products from each other. The Soviet Union is one of the leading grain buyers of the world and could be a leading buyer in almost any field, given the size of its population. The Soviet Union is one of the leading producers of oil and gold, and it could become a leading producer in other fields if it would concentrate its resources on what it can do relatively well, the way Japan has. The United States could sell grain and other products to the Soviet Union in return for gold, oil, and other products, thereby easing the international deficit, which can be paid in gold, and the U.S. energy problems.

Everything that is shown in Table 22-8 can be subjected to a computerized what-if analysis. Such an analysis enables one to determine what it would take to bring any of those alternatives that are tied for second place up to first place. It also enables one to determine the effects of adding additional goals, changing the alternatives, or changing any of the inputs. This kind of what-if capability may be the most important purpose that is served by working with decisionaiding software. Some of the benefits can also be obtained by working with a spreadsheet matrix (like that of Table 22-8 with alternatives, goals, relations, and total scores) even if the matrix is not computerized. One type of sensitivity analysis that is often especially helpful is to ask what would be the winning alternative if we just concentrate on the conservative goals or give them extra weight, which in this case would be having a higher GNP with full employment and lots of consumer goods. One exciting characteristic of super-optimum solutions is that they win even when one uses only conservative weights or only liberal weights. The reason here and often in other SOS situations is that the SOS alternative does better than the other alternatives on every individual goal, not just better on the overall total. There are ways of systematically arriving at super-optimum solutions. That, however, is partly a subject for Chapter 19 on "Broadening the Applicability of Multi-Criteria Dispute Resolution" and for my next book on *Super-Optimum Solutions in Public Controversies*.

SECTION C: POLITICAL HURDLES

Chapter 23

TYPES OF FEASIBILITY

I. SEVEN TYPES OF FEASIBILITY

There are at least eight potential feasibility obstacles that need to be taken into consideration in trying to move a win-win or super-optimum solution from a conceptual proposal through the political process into an adopted and implemented public policy. Those potential feasibility obstacles in random order include the following:

1. *Economic* feasibility first refers to whether there is *enough money* available to finance the alternative, e.g., health care, jobs for public aid recipients. For further details and examples, see Chapter 14 on "Economic Hurdles: Budget Hurdles."
2. *Economic* feasibility also refers to *displaced workers and firms*. Perhaps the most serious feasibility problem is what to do about workers and businesses who were displaced. They may be displaced as a result of such win-win approaches as (1) productivity downsizing, (2) civilian conversion, (3) free trade, (4) immigration, and (5) jobs for people who were formerly discriminated against such as minorities, women, disabled people, the elderly, and others. For further details and examples, see Chapter 15 on "Economic Hurdles: Displacement."
3. *Technological* feasibility refers to whether the alternative is capable of being developed in view of obstacles that relate to the principles of physical science, biological science, or other scientific principles, e.g., (1) environmental protection such as cleaner and less expensive processes, (2) energy sources such as safe nuclear or massive solar energy, and (3) an AIDS cure or vaccine. For further details and examples, see Chapter 16 on "Technology Hurdles."
4. S*ocial-Psychological feasibility* involves changing people's attitudes. For example, judicial review in England is not so needed where government officials and the public have a strong attitude toward compliance with constitutional principles. For another example, the best way to reduce sexual harassment is to increase respect for women starting with childhood socialization, rather than through regulations and penalties. For further details and examples, see Chapter 17on "Sociology-Psychology Hurdles."
5. Adoption or *political* feasibility first refers to whether the alternative is capable of being passed by a relevant legislature and not vetoed by the relevant president or

other chief executive, e.g., drug medicalization, on-site registration. For further details and examples, see Chapter 18 on "Political Science Hurdles: Politics."

6. *Political* feasibility also refers to implementation or *administrative* hurdles such as whether the alternative is capable of being monitored and enforced, e.g., toxic waste (standards and settlement), contracting out schools (test scores, drop-out rates, time needed). For further details and examples, see Chapter 19 on "Political Science Hurdles: Administration."
7. *International* feasibility. This is the kind of feasibility that needs to be met when a proposed super-optimum solution requires or would greatly benefit from some form of international cooperation. An example would be an international trade agreement like NAFTA or GATT. Such agreements are highly mutually beneficial, but often have hurdles to overcome regarding the anxieties of displaced workers and firms, psychological nationalism, or problems of administrative implementation. For further details and examples, see Chapter 20 on "International Hurdles."
8. *Constitutional* feasibility refers to whether the alternative is capable of being judged by the courts as being in conformity with the constitution. A related kind of feasibility is legal feasibility that refers to whether the alternative conforms with relevant statutes, administrative regulations, court precedents, or other applicable law besides the U.S. Constitution, for example (1) PAC or political action committee restrictions, (2) 'Don't ask, don't tell' in dealing with homosexuals in the military, and (3) public housing searches on the theory of implied consent. For further details and examples, see Chapter 20 on "International Hurdles."

II. Feasibility Types by Policy Problem

A. Abortion

One could take a single policy problem and show how any of the kinds of feasibility can apply such as the abortion problem. The SOS to the abortion controversy might emphasize greatly receiving unwanted pregnancies through better birth control and abstinence.

1. *Constitutional* feasibility means that the seeking of an outright prohibition on abortion at the state or Congressional level looks like it will not get passed in the Supreme Court.
2. *Political* or adoption feasibility might relate to the free choice bill like the Equal Rights Amendment. Congress will not touch it for fear of antagonizing too many emotional voters. They will also argue that there is no need to do so since the Supreme Court has provided for free choice and equal gender rights.
3. An example of *administrative* feasibility is trying to prohibit abortions and make it stick since back alley abortions do not seem capable of getting wiped out.
4. The *technological* feasibility might relate to coming up with a form of birth control that would not involve anything that would be considered unnatural. But could possibly be handled as a dietary matter. That may not be technologically feasible.
5. In developing nations the pill and even the condom lack *economic* feasibility.

B. Drug Crimes

1. *Constitutionally* unfeasible to provide the death penalty where there is no murder involved.
2. *Politically* unfeasible to talk about legalization at the present time.
3. *Administratively* unfeasible to cut off the supply.
4. No *technological* substitute for cocaine like methadone is for heroin.
5. The *economic* feasibility comes up in the context of whether we can afford cocaine treatment programs. They would be expensive but they would save a lot of money in comparison to the money that is spent in trying to cut off supply and trying to deal with drug-related crimes.

C. Health Care Legislation

There are about eight kinds of feasibility for health care legislation that should be addressed.

1. Economic Feasibility: Lack of Budget

The program had a drop from 100% to 95% and possibly 92% because there is not enough money available for subsidies that would guarantee 100% coverage. The subsidy idea in the form of a voucher is a win-win approach, meaning a partial subsidy, or more important, meaning a certificate that entities one to buy a private sector product. The trouble with how economic feasibility is handled in health care is that it never addressed the possibility of getting enough money by a reallocation from other governmental activities. Defense, drug enforcement, or paying interest on the debt. It only talked about reallocation of health care expenses, like diverting money wasted on Medicare and Medicaid. It is also not politically feasible to raise income taxes, but acceptable to raise cigarette taxes. That did not provide enough.

On economic feasibility, there may not be enough money to cover the subsidies to have universal coverage if the government has to rely on a cigarette tax and tax on luxury health care programs. The whole health care universality, may be in jeopardy unless Clinton can get through the employer mandate or come up with a tax Increase to make up the difference. For further details, see Section II "The Example of Health Care" in Chapter 14 on "Economic Hurdles: Budget Hurdles."

2. Economic Feasibility: Displaced Workers

This includes fee-for-service doctors and other health care workers who cannot compete with HMOs. Many of the fee-for-service doctors, or at least the better ones, have been invited to join HMOs. Likewise, nursing homes and private hospitals have been increasingly participating in the HMO movement. In discussing the politics of health care policy, we do note that private-sector insurance companies are now frequently providing the insurance work for HMOs, and private-sector pharmaceutical companies are working closely with HMOs to their joint profitable benefits.

3. Technology Feasibility

On all of these we could compare health care legislation with environmental. That gets too complicated. Better to stick with just one policy subject in order to illustrate the different kinds of feasibility. There are technology problems in trying to develop new ways of manufacturing that are both cleaner and more profitable. Health care is not so designed to develop any new technologies. It is designed to spread existing technologies to people who otherwise cannot afford them. It is up to the HMOs to decide which existing technologies get included. The government may specify a certain minimum of coverage, like x-rays for lung problems once a year, but CAT scans only under specified circumstances. The HMOs compete in the services they offer. The more important incentive to use modern diagnostic technology is to decrease the treatment cost.

On technological feasibility, there is nothing technologically difficult or complicated. New medical technologies are covered by HMOs unless they are extremely exotic and expensive. One can obtain the latest kinds of biomedical technology, including various kinds of transplants, all kinds of MRAs and CAT scans, although not unnecessary MRAs, and not technologies that have not yet been reasonably well developed, like brain transplants. It used to be a joke to talk about penis transplants. The Bobbitt case shows that it can be done by an HMOs almost as an outpatient basis at a very low cost. That is a very dramatic form of modern technology. Also on the business side one might note that the HMOs can make use of the latest computerized recordkeeping, invoicing, medical diagnosis, all of which may involve computers. They can do it better than a small fee for service doctor's office.

4. Social-Psychological Feasibility

People sometimes confuse the group practice of HMOs with collectivism or socialism, especially if encouraged to do so by fee-for-service doctors and traditional insurance companies. What is needed in that regard is better communication on the part of the Clinton Administration or others who are pushing related health care programs. The communication needs to make clear that HMOs are private sector doctors and hospitals. They are not doctors on salary to the government or government hospitals. A government hospital might be included in an HMO program, such as where a private HMO allows a patient to go to a doctor at a government hospital such as the Cook County Hospital.

5. Political Feasibility: Politics

Political feasibility in terms of getting through Congress or some other legislature and getting the president's signature. We can use the health care bill as an illustrative example. It lacked political feasibility because of the employer mandate arousing too much opposition. The mandate should have been dropped and instead emphasizing low cost quality health insurance that employers and others would want to voluntarily buy. The mandate idea is traditional regulation. Talking in terms of incentives is a more modern win-win approach. The environmental field is an even better example than health care.

It has political feasibility given strong opposition from businesses that do not want to pay the mandate, Also, fee for service doctors who do not like the HMOs competition. Also, insurance companies who also do not like the HMOs. Also, pharmaceuticals and other health care providers which have to compete with HM0s. They are all afraid that the alliances, which are designed to represent health care consumers and get as good a health care insurance deal as possible will choose the HMOs because they are so obviously better on both cost and quality. That motivation behind the opposition has never been communicated by the Clinton people. Instead they have tried to appease the opposition by de-emphasizing the HMOs. Clinton is trying to communicate to the public about the crime bill and maybe a little about health care, but he has some big political feasibility problems when public opinion is so far off as to what both kinds of legislation provide for, especially health care. For further details, see Section III "Health Care Policy" in Chapter 18 on "Political Science Hurdles: Politics."

6. Political Feasibility: Administrative

Administrative feasibility could be a big problem if the government were to own and operate health care facilities. It is being delegated to the private sector, especially the HMOs. There are still administrative problems though, in trying to decide who is eligible for a subsidy. The criteria need to be worked out. Anybody with family income per person above a certain amount gets no subsidy. The figure for the poverty line is about $14,000 for a family of four. The figure for a health care subsidy should be about twice that, meaning $28,000 for a family of four. Any family earning less than that would be eligible for a subsidy. A chart would be needed to indicate how much of a subsidy. If the family income is only $14,000, then 100% subsidy because that would be like Medicaid. $21,000 is a 50% subsidy. One could work out a formula for using simple extrapolation: 14 is 100%, 28 is %, 21 is 50%, and so on for the other amounts. We do not need to go through the interpolation formula. This is just designed to show that there is an administrative problem, but it is feasible.

On administrative feasibility, there is an argument that the situation will be very difficult to administer because it covers so many people and so many health care providers and treatments. The administration though, is primarily through HMOs. They are generally well managed. That is part of what is meant by managed competition. It is not administration by some kind of socialized medicine with government doctors. That kind of a system does tend to get very sloppy because the salaried government doctors do not have adequate incentives for efficient administration. The HMOs do. Any waste on their part cuts into their profits and salaries.

7. International Feasibility

An example of international feasibility in the health care field is the AIDS problem and other diseases that are especially rampant among impoverished developing nations. The problem is that although those countries may be international-law abiding, they cannot afford the high prices for anti-AIDS drugs. As a result, they encourage private-sector pirating or the government itself manufactures low-price anti-AIDS drugs. Contrary to WTO and international trade agreements, that kind of hurdle is being increasingly overcome by allowing emergency exceptions to those trade rules or by pharmaceutical companies voluntarily donating anti-AIDS drugs free or at low prices. It should also be noted that the pharmaceuticals have a fantastically profitable markup on their drugs which interferes with their obtaining sympathy from world public opinion. The *New York Times* in December, 2000, ran an article on a pharmaceutical firm in India that profitably sells lifesaving pharmaceuticals often at less than one tenth of the manufacturer's requested price. They are willing to pay a reasonable royalty to the pharmaceutical companies, but they are not willing to give the companies close to 100% of sales.

8. Constitutional Feasibility

Constitutional feasibility is not so much an issue in-the current legislation, but it could be if there are still important class differences left. The legislation is designed to lessen those differences. That is what universality is all about. It is universality in terms of people covered, though, not treatment covered. Some treatments will still only be available to the rich. That has never successfully raised the constitutional issue It should be noted, though, that legal services available only to the rich are unconstitutional. Poor people are entitled to free legal help in criminal cases by way of the Sixth Amendment, but there is no clause about free medical help to the poor or to the middle class.

On legal and constitutional feasibility, there is nothing questionable in this legislation. The closest thing might be if people are denied certain treatments, would the denial be considered an arbitrary classification contrary to the equal protection clause. The answer is definitely yes if the denial is based on race, gender, or economic class, or region. Economic class could come up. A certain kind of bypass or heart transplant may only be available to rich people. The HMO contract would probably specify that nobody gets that kind of bypass whether they are rich or poor under the $2,000/year insurance. A rich person can go to a private fee for service doctor and get the treatment outside of the insurance, and pay his own money. That may have some elements of unfairness and inequity, but it is not government discrimination. The courts have never held that the government has an obligation to do any equalizing like that. The government has an obligation to provide lawyers to the poor, but not doctors, especially not doctors for highly expensive surgery, but not even doctors for anything. There is no constitutional right to medicine, but if the government does provide medical treatment to some people it cannot arbitrarily exclude others with arbitrary meaning based on race, gender, class, or region. The government cannot discriminate, but the government does not have to equalize when there is discrimination in the private sector.

Some business firm might argue that forcing it to pay is like taking private property without just compensation. The court doesn't see that as a constitutional problem. The government has a right to force people to pay taxes so long as doing so is not discriminatory. The element of force in a non-discriminatory way does not raise constitutional issues. Forcing someone to give up property they own does mean being compensated, but not forcing the payment of taxes.

Chapter 24

FEASIBILITY OF DIVERSE PROPOSALS

I. JURY DECISION-MAKING AS A DETAILED EXAMPLE

A. Feasibility

We can go down the list of feasibility aspects as a good checklist. On political feasibility, this is not a matter on which Democrats or Republicans are divided. On economic feasibility, the cost is low and money would be saved since stenotypists cost more than videotaping.

On administrative feasibility it is just a matter of setting up a permanent videotape machine in the back of the courtroom that can see and hear. It would have a six-hour tape and not have to be changed very often. There could be some kind of an alarm that goes off if it is not working. The worst scenario is that the machine breaks down and nobody knows about it and thus part of the trial is not recorded. No harm is done unless somebody appeals and needs a transcript. If that happens, then a new trial would have to be ordered. Thus, we would not want an alarm because the loser would always appeal knowing that a new trial would be granted. Maybe it could be a silent alarm that rings in a court clerk's office who then comes in quietly and replaces the machine. The technology is there, although it did not exist previously.

In terms of constitutionality it is not like having disruptive television cameras. This would be no more obtrusive and maybe less so than a stenotypist. Even television in the courtroom has been upheld as not disruptive to a fair trial. Psychological feasibility is the temporary obstacle. This means just plain inertia. For example, a stenotypist took down everything that was said at the city council hearing. It could have been done easier with a videotape, with more accuracy in terms of seeing and hearing what was going on and getting all the words accurately without ad-libbing or the cost of transcribing.

Regarding displaced workers, some stenotypists would be out of jobs. Maybe they could still use their skills in taking depositions, but these can be done with videotaping too. Stenotypists' skills could be used in taking dictation, although there is no instant replay. Lots of downsizing occurs as a result of new technologies. This would be an example. There should be programs for retraining that also involve job placement, wage subsidies, and day care. People should not be retained in favor of a procedure that costs less and gets a better quality product. Provision should be made to facilitate displaced workers getting new jobs.

B. Devil's Advocate Points

What about the cost of videotaping? The initial costs of the machine or the tapes are not very high. The cost of running the machine is less than a stenotypist. It may require no operator.

What about stenotypists being out of jobs? There are plenty of opportunities for stenotypists to work in offices, including doing dictation typing.

There is still a need for answering the question as to what the jury size should be. We do not want to evade that question. The jury size can be anything between 6 and 12, supplemented by videotaping, notetaking, and other approaches to improve the accuracy of jury decision making.

Why has videotaping not yet been adopted? It is a relatively new technology. There has been more concentration on the trade-off controversy as far as jury size is concerned. And videotaping has been viewed as a money saver rather than for improving accuracy.

There are other approaches to the 6-person versus 12-person jury problem. One could rely on anecdotes, which tend to say there is no difference.

In states that have 6-person juries the law may make it easier to convict. Or the people may be different or the cases may be different. The problem is not solved by just comparing with more states.

The approach of relying on experimental juries is defective because it might depend too much on a single case that could be biased. It might require videotaping 50 trials and playing them to 50 12-person juries and 50 6-person juries, which would be too expensive.

A deductive model may be helpful but it has the defect of emphasizing trade perspectives and possibly faulty assumptions.

II. Minimum Wage as a Detailed Example

A. Feasibility

From a political feasibility perspective, we can think in terms of seven sets of people who represent potential opposition, including three groups on the left, three on the right, and the general public in the middle. There are four benefits to the general public: (1) the money saved from otherwise providing public aid to unemployed people; (2) the money added to the gross national product, which increases taxes and provides income to others and an increased base on which to grow in subsequent years; (3) better role models for the children of people who would otherwise be unemployed; and (4) an upgrading of skills if qualifying for the wage subsidy means business has to provide on-the-job training and workers have to participate. It is clear how workers and employers in the program benefit. Other workers can join and other employers can join. It is open-access. On the general left is a feeling that this is a handout to business and abuses the workers with subminimum wages. The answer to that is the workers are being paid more than the minimum and business is not getting a handout. Businesses provide a quid pro quo in the form of hiring unemployed workers and providing on-the-job training (OJT), which they would not do without the program. On the right it could look like a handout to the unemployed, like public aid. The answer to this is that the workers have to work and do well enough (not to be fired) on the job and in the training program.

The key question then is why hasn't the system been more widely adopted. The key answer is that it costs money, meaning there are economic feasibility problems. Even though the payoff may be substantially more than the money invested, the money may still not be appropriated. The difficulty of getting policies funded that have future payoffs can be indicated by the news items on tax cuts rather than using the state surpluses for investment purposes. Economic feasibility relates to both adoption and implementation. The program may never get adopted in view of the unwillingness to appropriate the money.

There may be some administrative problems, but not many because the program is delegated to private-sector employers. It is not the kind of administrative program that requires any complicated tax collecting or imaginative discretion. All the employers have to do is hire people who were otherwise unemployed and provide them with OJT, which after six months should enable them to get off the subsidy and be worth the current or raised minimum wage. This could be a one-year program. The administrative agency might be the unemployment compensation offices or the jobs program offices. This is private-sector employment, though, not working for government agencies where administrative problems can ruin the program, especially since government employers have no profit motive and may be willing to hire relatively unproductive people just to provide them with jobs. The private sector is not going to do that. The productivity aspect is in a sense self-enforcing.

On the matter of technology, one reason for unemployment is that new technologies displace workers. Another technology aspect is that OJT may especially lead to trained workers who can handle the new technologies.

There is no constitutional problem. It is not an arbitrary classification of people to say only unemployed people are eligible for these minimum wage subsidies. They represent greater hardship cases than those who already have jobs. It might be more meaningful to use the minimum wage instead of switching to health care or maybe even both.

B. Sources of Opposition

The key feasibility question is political feasibility, especially support for the voucher from the general public and from management and labor. Labor could be divided into the workers who are covered by the vouchers and other workers. There is also opposition from a general right wing and a general left wing that are broader than the immediate employers and workers.

The general public benefits from the strings attached to the vouchers, which require management to hire unemployed workers and provide OJT. Workers are required to take the job and the training and to perform acceptably. This results in saving taxes and various forms of public aid that would otherwise go to the unemployed workers. Other benefits to the general public include adding to the GNP as a result of doing productive work, which has multiplier effects for many other people who receive income as a result of the spending, and also by paying taxes on income received. This makes money available to cover the vouchers. Also, there is the positive role model for one's children or grandchildren. There are lower costs from a reduction in antisocial activities that are associated with people being unemployed. The positive role models are an intergenerational effect. There is also a compounding effect if taxes are paid, which enables the taxes to be considered like interest on the increased national debt so that the government has the money available for reinvestment. That's like interest on the increment, which leads to further growth.

Other workers are also eligible for OJT so that they can increase their productivity and wages. The workers in the program are getting jobs and training. The employers are getting workers at less than the minimum wage, with their training being increased. The workers are getting paid more than the minimum wage. The right wing might object on the grounds that this is a handout program, but it is not. The unemployed workers have to perform well on the job and in the training program or else they get fired. We can think of the opposition as being the general left (intellectual liberals rather than workers), other workers, workers in the program, general public, employers in the program, other employers, and general right (intellectual conservatives rather than employers). That's seven possible sources of opposition. A good political feasibility analysis should take all of them into consideration.

Other employers who might object can always enter the program, although they may not want to hire workers that are so unskilled. This kind of program, though, could be used for any level of skill. A worker who is a lawyer, who would otherwise get paid maybe $100/hr, but who is unemployed, could get a wage supplement. This means that if the supplement is worth 20% of the market price and the market price is $ 100, then in theory the government pays $20 and the employer pays $80 in order to provide an incentive to hire the unemployed lawyer. In practice, wage supplements make sense mainly or exclusively for people who are unemployed who need a wage supplement in order to make them employable at the minimum wage. We have plenty of people like that, or close to it, who are on public aid or displaced workers due to tariff reduction, downsizing, defense conversion, or other reasons. The program needs to concentrate on people who would otherwise be on public aid. Unemployed lawyers and doctors are not likely to be on public aid. The unemployed lawyer can go to work generally at well above the minimum wage by doing nonlaw work for a business firm. The unemployed public aid recipient does not have much in the way of options. He may have no employer willing to hire him without a subsidy. The term "subsidy," though, should not be used in referring to these minimum wage vouchers. The worker is not getting a handout, but is doing a job. Likewise the employer is not getting a handout for hiring somebody who does nonsense work.

The general left-wing opposition does not like the idea of a substandard minimum wage or handouts to business. But this is not a substandard minimum wage, since the workers are getting paid more than the minimum wage, except the government is making up the difference. It is also not a handout to business. They are agreeing to provide jobs to workers who would otherwise be unemployed, and to provide on-the-job training. It all adds up to a good example of a win-win solution that takes into consideration lots of different sources of opposition and political feasibility. It also illustrates the mechanics of a scoring process. In terms of a what-if analysis, one might raise the question as to whether this would be a win-win solution if management were allowed to pay only $3 an hour and the workers were to get $7 an hour. This would mean a supplement of a lot more than $4 an hour and would no longer be an SOS, because the taxpayers would be paying out a lot more than they would be getting back in terms of less public aid and other benefits, especially the saving on taxes. These workers would be paying taxes on what they earn, but substantially less than what they would be receiving.

C. Devil's Advocate Positions

If the management side refuses to pay more than about $1 an hour and the labor side demands about $7 an hour, then the supplement would be $6.02 an hour and the general public would definitely not be getting its money's worth. Thus, the system works only if the gap between the conservative and liberal sides is small enough so that the wage supplement, or the rent supplement in the case of landlords and tenants, can be cost effective. This means that the cost is not so high that it exceeds the benefits that the general public would be receiving in terms of increased productivity on the part of otherwise unemployed people.

If the unemployed workers receive a supplement that causes their wages to exceed the previously employed workers who are doing the same kind of work, then those previously employed workers are going to feel rather resentful.

The newly employed workers are required to enter into an OJT program that the previous workers are not required to enter. The previous workers, though, may consider being in that program to be a benefit, not a cost. They should also therefore have access to the program if they want to be in it.

The previously employed workers are probably going to demand and succeed in getting a wage increase. It would be hard for management to justify paying the previous workers less than the new workers if they are doing the same work. The justification that management would offer would be that it is the government's money, not management money. It would be difficult for the government then to justify paying extra money for the same type of work.

In reality, there are not likely to be very many workers who are making just barely above the minimum wage to complain. The workers who are most likely to complain are unionized workers who make substantially more than the minimum wage. They have the most capability of complaining successfully because they are organized, but they are not likely to have anything to complain about since their wages are already substantially higher than the minimum wage.

Also, even the workers whose wages are substantially higher are in a better position now to demand still higher wages if people are being brought in at a new higher figure. This has a buoying-up effect on wages further up the line.

Workers should always welcome new workers being brought in at extremely high wages because it tends to raise the wage scale of the previous workers. The disparity is only temporary. Academics who are not short-sighted welcome their department adding a few new faculty members at $100,000 or $200,000 apiece in view of that buoying-up effect. Or in this case, it would be a pulling up, rather than a pushing up effect.

Another argument made against the minimum wage supplement is that it forces on an employer relatively incompetent aged people, disabled people, mothers of preschool children, and the traditionally unemployed.

However, it does not force anything on anybody. No employer has to accept the subsidy. The employer is paying from his pocket less than the minimum wage, in recognition of the fact that these people may (until they receive further training) not be as competent as previous employees. The OJT may make them even more competent than the previous employees.

The employer may object on the grounds that OJT is too expensive to provide. The government is in effect paying for part of it by way of the subsidy. This is a rather shortsighted position, since OJT will make the workers more productive and thereby enable the employer to get more out of them and thus make better profits in the long run, which may occur very quickly.

The workers may object that they do not like having to be in an OJT program. They can quit. Nobody is forcing them to be in the program. This is not a criminal sentence. If they do not want to receive the subsidy, they can go back to doing whatever they had been doing previously. Most workers, though, would welcome the opportunity to take on a subsidized job with free OJT, especially where completing the training means that one moves into a higher-paying job category.

This is not a program designed to solve all the problems of unemployment and a lack of updated worker skills. It is a minimum-wage policy in recognition of the fact that some workers may not be worth the minimum wage, at least in the eyes of the employer, unless their skills are upgraded. It is also a recognition of the fact that if the government is going to give out a subsidy to workers and employers, it may as well ask for some useful strings or repayment in the forms of hiring the unemployed and offering and accepting on-the-job training.

There may be some objection from people who feel that this is a reward to lazy people who are unemployed. This is a matter of semantics. It is an incentive to accept a job and OJT, it is not a reward. One could even view it as a form of punishment if one emphasizes the obligation to accept employment in return for public aid. It makes more sense to emphasize the opportunity to have employment and OJT. There are those who feel that the way to deal with unemployment is to punish the unemployed rather than to provide incentives to the unemployed to get jobs, and especially to potential employers to hire them. This punishment attitude might be considered not a major viewpoint that a super-optimum solution needs to appease, but it just happens that it does help to satisfy it by presenting the policy to such conservative audiences as a workfare program rather than a job opportunity program.

Chapter 25

CAUSAL ANALYSIS IN SOS ADOPTION AND IMPLEMENTATION

I. THINKING ABOUT THE CONCEPT OF SOS PREDICTION

An SOS is a policy alternative in which both liberal and conservative come out ahead of their initial best expectations. It implies a normative analysis as to what alternative should be adopted. In dealing with SOS prediction, we are talking about what alternative will be adopted or why an alternative was adopted rather than what should be adopted.

They are closely related in the following senses:

1. In order to decide what should be adopted, we should show some awareness of what can be or will be under various circumstances. We should not recommend impossible alternatives.
2. If we want to explain why an alternative was adopted, it is best to do so in terms of what the participants, or decision-makers think should be adopted, or what they thought should have been adopted. That also means taking their goals into consideration in order to predict or explain.
3. Thus, prescription makes use of prediction in order to prescribe. Likewise, prediction makes use of prescription in order to predict.

An ordinary prediction differs from an SOS prediction in the following ways.

1. An SOS prediction may be concerned with predicting what SOS alternative will be adopted, and especially whether an SOS alternative will be adopted or whether the SOS alternative will be adopted.
2. It can also involve an attempt to explain why some situations lead to SOS alternatives and others do not.

II. Causal Analysis of SOS Adoption

A. Up the Ante

One phenomenon that may tend to occur more with an SOS than with an ordinary solution is that after the solution has been suggested, each side feels the other side is getting such a good deal that each side tends to up the ante by increasing their demands. That is an aspect of the psychology of super-optimum solutions. Each side should really do just the opposite. Each side should say, I am getting such a good deal that I should not be so demanding or else the whole thing might fall through.

An example is a labor dispute. The attorney for the farm workers was bothered by the fact that the growers were getting off lightly, regardless how much the farm workers might be benefiting. As a result, he came up with new demands that were not mentioned before.

We could name this the Mazmanian phenomenon in honor of Daniel Mazmanian's saying that he does not care how much Nagel is doing for the Policy Studies Organization, Nagel is benefiting too much himself. That is the phenomenon in dispute resolution where people are not so oriented toward maximizing their side. The Mazmanian-type person is marching to a different drummer in which a key goal is keeping down the benefits of other people in the dispute resolution situation. This is also the age-old phenomenon of cutting off one's body to spite one's head or some variation thereon whereby one suffers great costs in order to see to it that the other side does not get any benefits. It is a mindset that tends to view dispute resolution as being a defeat if the other person comes out ahead.

That did not occur in the Sanyo case. To the extent that the Sanyo case super-optimum solution was disrupted, it was not because the lawyers for the plaintiff wanted to see the Sanyo company hurt or did not want to see it benefit. The Sanyo case had virtually no emotion to it at all compared to the class, ideological, and personal conflict of the Ramirez case. The lawyers for the plaintiff in the Sanyo case did not like the SOS because they did not want to be paid off in computers, television sets, insurance claims, or annuities. They wanted cash. They therefore preferred the old-fashioned splitting the dollars difference. They would then take their one-third and go home. Therefore, a key implementation problem has to do with disputants in dispute resolution situations being represented by outsiders such as lawyers. Their interests may not be the same as the disputants. They may not be so interested in implementing an SOS that would benefit the disputants because the solution does not benefit them sufficiently over a traditional solution and may even be worse than a traditional solution.

B. Representatives

Try to make sure that not only do the disputants come out ahead of their best expectations, but also their representatives. If their representatives do not come out so well, then they may present a bad roadblock toward implementing the SOS. In the Sanyo case, one thing that could have been done was to provide for cash side-payments. The Sanyo Company was not willing to do that. That would defeat the SOS if they had to pay a lot of cash to a plaintiff's lawyer, as contrasted to giving low-cost computers or television sets to the plaintiff.

Another solution is to make it explicit as part of the agreement that the plaintiff (Traveller's Insurance Company) will gladly pay a cash payment to the plaintiffs lawyer in view of the benefits that the plaintiff is getting. If the plaintiff is getting one million dollars worth of computers and television sets, they would not necessarily pay one-third of a million in cash to the lawyer, but at least one-third of half the $900, 000 which was the plaintiffs original best expectation. The most the lawyers expected to get was probably $150,000, which would be one third of $450,000 if the demand would only be cut in half if the defendant were offering zero. If the defendant were offering $300,000, then $1,200,000 is cut in half meaning a $600,000 settlement, and the plaintiffs lawyers get $200,000 or one-third of that The Traveler's Insurance Company would still come out ahead even if they gave their lawyer one-third of $900,000, or $300,000. They would still have $700,000 worth of computers, plus insurance claims worth maybe more than the $300,000. The important point is that explicit attention has to be paid to how the plaintiffs lawyer is going to be compensated and not just how the plaintiff is going to be compensated.

C. Regardless How Well the Other Side Does

A second key point is to somehow educate both sides into seeking to maximize their own benefits minus costs, regardless how well the other side does. That should not be so hard to do even if one side considers it a benefit to make the other side suffer or deprive the other side of benefits. Surely even people with that point of view would value receiving benefits themselves directly, as being worth more than the indirect satisfaction of depriving the other side of benefits.

One can say that the lawyer in the Ramirez case may be messing things up more than the plaintiff clients. The lawyer may be feeling more emotionally upset than the plaintiffs are. That is partly an ego thing. Lawyers sometimes tend to have big egos, and maybe even more so with lawyers who represent migrant labor. They may have a tendency to view themselves as the great white father coming to free the slaves and have all kinds of complexes about their importance. The labor lawyer in that case did indicate he was having problems with regard to ego and status matters that should have been considered more. He was especially bothered by such things as the defendant's lawyer talking longer. Defendants do need to be brought around in a more time-consuming way than plaintiffs. It is the defendants who have to give and the plaintiffs who receive.

D. Suspicion that a Trap is Involved

The Camp David Accord almost fell apart as a result of suspicion that a trap was involved. The passage of time tends to cure that, although the agreement had to be reached before the passage of time could occur.

E. Removing Versus Adding Goals

An SOS may sometimes be more readily found or implemented by subtracting a goal rather than adding one. That is true if one side is especially interested in Goal X in which the other side is negative or not interested. If Goal X is dividing them, then removing it as a goal may facilitate a solution. Normally, adding more goals provides each side with a package of things it can receive which it values, and the other side with a package of things it can receive which the first side does not consider as giving up very much. The package solution is a most meaningful SOS approach, and it involves multi-criteria thinking.

If A rejects an SOS solution because B will also benefit, then that is a form of spitefulness. If A fails to think toward an SOS solution because gain by B is perceived to mean a loss by A, then that may be unduly narrow thinking. It can result in missed opportunities to find ways in which both A and B can benefit. An example is the opposition of the American Society for Public Administration to marketing journals of its sections to libraries for fear that doing so will detract from the marketing of the Public Administration Review. It might, however, be quite possible that a marketing program could be developed in which PAR and the section journals could both come out ahead.

F. Vested Jobs and Property as an Obstacle to SOS Adoption

A big problem in replacing a traditional compromise with an SOS solution is there may already be vested jobs or property in the previous decision, they to be taken into consideration. An example is that both conservatives and liberals strongly endorse rent supplements over public housing projects. Conservatives do so partly because rent supplements represent a marketplace solution to housing for the poor. Liberals do so partly because rent supplements facilitate integration along economic and racial lines. The rent supplement program has, however, not replaced public housing.

A big part of the explanation is the vested jobs and property in the previous solution. Public housing was previously supported by liberals as a form of equitable socialism. It has been tolerated by conservatives as an approach to housing for the poor which would not involve integration at a time when integration was less acceptable. Neither of those original purposes have much explanatory value for the retention of public housing over a rent supplements program, but the existence of vested jobs and property does.

The key question is not what explains why the SOS solution has not been fully adopted, but rather what to do about that kind of interfering factor. The traditional compromise approach is a variation on grandfathering or a tolerated zoning use. Such a solution means that no new public housing projects are built but the old ones are allowed to die of old age. It also means that people holding jobs under the old system are allowed to retain them, but a minimum of replacement occurs when the former jobholders die, retire, or resign.

An SOS solution that relies more on well-placed subsidies would phase out the property as quickly as possible, rather than wait for nature obsolescence. A fast phase-out though would not mean a wasteful dynamiting of the public housing projects as was done with the Pruitt-Igoe Homes in St. Louis. Instead, the projects could be made available along with appropriate subsidies for use a factories, warehouses, or other buildings as part of an inner-city Enterprise Zone project which is an SOS in itself. The jobholders could also be provided with well-placed subsidies for retraining, buying small businesses, or other alternative activities that fit their skills.

This problem of what to do about vested jobs and property comes up in many SOS situations, such as tariff reduction which can be highly mutually beneficial internationally. Adequate provision needs to be made for people and property that have a vested interest in the previous, less beneficial activities.

III. Causes of Successful and Unsuccessful SOS Implementation

A. Clarifying SOS Success

The concept of super-optimum solutions has not been around as a formal concept for very long. It is possible that even in prehistoric times, two people may have argued over something and resolved their dispute in such a way that they both came out better than their initial best expectations. The idea as a formal concept probably did not get articulated until about the 1950's with the development of game theory in mathematics, operations research, and management science. The typical game or human interaction studied involved a relatively fixed pie in which the gains of one side were equal to the losses of the other side. Thus these were referred to as zero-sum games because the combined results for both sides added to zero. Game theorists mentioned non-zero-sum games, where both sides (or all sides) could come out ahead, as contrasted to a winner and a loser. However, they developed virtually no literature on the subject.

The idea of all sides coming out ahead (or at least not taking a loss) was actually formalized as a concept in the early 1900's by Vilfredo Pareto. That is the concept of the Pareto Optimum. For Pareto, it was a measurement concept. He never discussed causal factors for bringing it about, or for explaining variance as to why it sometimes exists and sometimes does not in human interaction. His concept is also a very weak one in the sense that one could devise a policy for a billion inhabitants of China in which nobody gains or loses except one person who gains one unit. That would be classified as a Pareto Optimum. Common sense though might say that surely one could do better than that, and such a result thus does not deserve to be called an optimum except in an arbitrary definitional sense, rather than in empirically observing how people use concepts like best, optimum, or even good.

In the 1970's alternative dispute resolution began to acquire popularity among lawyers, business people, union leaders, and others. It basically meant resolving disputes by alternatives other than going to court where one side wins and the other side loses. The original motivation for going to an alternative arbitrator or mediator (rather than a judge) was partly to avoid delay. Later, more emphasis was put on the purpose of achieving win-win solutions where everybody comes out ahead. Coming out ahead, though, tended to mean nothing more than coming out better than one's worst expectations.

Thus in a damages suit if the plaintiff demanded $100,000 and the defendant refused to offer more than $20,000, one might consider a $60,000 settlement as being a win-win settlement. The plaintiff could have received nothing as a result of losing on the liability issue, and the defendant could have wound up paying $100,000, rather than $60,000. Under more recent structured settlements, the plaintiff might receive $10,000 a year for every year over age 60 which would be worth more than $100,000 in the calculations of the plaintiff. The same arrangement could be worth possible less than $20,000 in the calculations of the defendant insurance company by way of its actuarial calculations and its depositing a reserve that draws compound interest to establish an endowment or annuity until the payments need to be made. that is more truly a super-optimum solution.

In the 1980's, super-optimizing took on a more meaningful form than the Pareto measurement concept, the non-zero-sum game, or the win-win dispute resolution. The new more meaningful form in the field of public policy was supply-side economics of the Reagan administration and economists like Arthur Laffer, along with industrial policy of such opposition candidates as Gary Hart and economists like Robert Reich. The emphasis in both perspectives is on the idea of the expanded pie or gross national product where all major viewpoints can come out ahead of their best expectations largely through well-placed subsidies and tax breaks.

A good example relates to dealing with the national deficit. Traditional conservatives argue in favor of reducing domestic spending and increasing taxes on consumers like the value-added tax. The traditional liberals argue for reducing defense spending and increasing taxes on the rich like the progressive income tax. both the SOS conservatives associated with supply-side economics and the SOS liberals associated with industrial policy tend to argue that the best way to reduce the deficit may be to increase spending, but spending that will stimulate increased productivity and thus increase the GNP which is the tax base. One can then obtain more tax income to reduce the deficit even with a constant or lowered tax rate. Both sides also argue that the deficit might be better dealt with by reducing some kinds of taxes where doing so is a tax break designed to stimulate increased productivity in a manner similar to a well-placed spending subsidy.

B. Some Experiences of the Reagan Administration

Thus going into the 1980's under the Reagan administration, the United States served as a partial laboratory to try these new super-optimizing ideas of supply-side Reaganomics to see how well they would work in enabling all major segments of the population to come out ahead of their best expectations. Even those who have favorable attitudes toward the Reagan administration will generally concede that Reaganomics did not do as well as expected. It certainly did not increase the GNP beyond inflation enough to reduce the deficit. In fact, the deficit during the eight years of the Reagan administration tripled in the sense that the per capita deficit as of 1988 was three times what it was as of 1980. That also means that as of about 1984, President Reagan had succeeded in incurring more of an accumulated national debt than all the previous presidents put together by causing the national debt to double even on a per capita basis.

What went wrong with the idea that well-placed subsidies and tax breaks could stimulate productivity and the GNP enough so that we could have more spending, lower taxes, less deficit, and a higher standard of living simultaneously'? As a matter of hindsight, there seem to be three key causal factors which can serve as a learning experience for improving future SOS policy-making and implementation. The first factor is that well-placed subsidies and tax breaks require that strings be attached in the sense of a quid pro quo in return for the subsidy or tax break that will be likely to result in increased national productivity. The 30% across-the-board tax cut was the opposite of that. It had no strings attached or quid pro quo. The reasoning was that somehow the invisible hand of laissez-faire capitalism would guide the money saved from not having to pay taxes into improving the technology of U.S. steel making, automobile manufacturing, and other industries.

Instead, the money saved went disproportionately into three relatively unproductive uses. One was real estate, largely for speculative purposes. Buying real estate for the purpose of building a new modernized factory can add to national productivity. Buying real estate for the purpose of waiting for a highway to go through or urban sprawl to come by does nothing for national productivity. The second unproductive use was luxury goods. It is interesting to note that as of 1980, the only long distance area codes in the United States were on land. After the 30% tax cut, the quantity of yachts with telephones became so great off the Atlantic coast and the Pacific coast that two new area codes had to be established just for all the yachts using their cellular telephones. The third relatively unproductive purpose was high executive salaries for American corporate executives bearing little relation to the extent to which they had improved the market share of their companies. General Motors is a good example where the annual salary of the chief executive rose multiple times while their market share drastically decreased in favor of Toyota and other Japanese manufacturers whose salaries are a fraction of the CEO salary at General Motors.

Tax cuts that might have made a lot more sense could have included not a 30% tax cut to US Steel, but a 60% tax cut or even 100% tax cut, meaning no obligation to pay any income taxes for the time period covered. The key aspect is not the size of the tax cut but rather the requirement that US Steel in return for the tax cut introduce more oxygenated steel making which is more competitive than traditional blast furnaces. Getting US Steel to do so may have required substantially more than a 30% tax cut, but with that kind of string attached. It might have required a 200% tax cut whereby US Steel would figure out what taxes it owed and then the U.S. government would pay that amount to US Steel rather than vice versa. That would in effect be a subsidy, though, rather than a tax cut. US Steel does have a great deal of trouble getting needed capital for adopting new technologies ever since it has been put into competition with Japanese, German, and Scandinavian steel and had to respond competitively.

The second big causal factor that interfered with the successful implementation of supply-side economics in the Reagan administration was that where strings were attached, the amount of money needed to get the strings accepted was too small. A good example was the Enterprise Zones idea. Its basic feature was offering inducements to private enterprise to locate or relocate in the inner city in order to provide productive employment opportunities for people who might otherwise be unemployed and a drain on the taxpayer and the deficit. The idea was partly borrowed from the British Labor Party and the Carter administration to the credit of the Reagan administration in being receptive to new ideas. The size of the subsidies, however, were too small to offer much of an inducement. Insult was added to cheapness by attempting to offer business firms partial exemptions from economic regulations governing minimum wages, maximum hours, child labor, equal employment, environmental protection, workplace safety, and whatever other regulations could be relaxed, but Congress would not go along with that. The amount of money for the 30% tax cut was huge, but no strings attached. The Enterprise zones had lots of strings attached as to what the business firms were to do in employing people, but the amount of money was to paltry.

The third causal factor needed for successful implementation is to have people who are skilled in knowing the technical aspects of a well-placed subsidy or tax break versus money down the drain. A good example of the lack of concern for that causal element is in the grants of the Department of Housing and Urban Development in the 1980's. Those grants had big money behind them and lots of strings attached. The grants had potential for contracting for meaningful scattered-site housing and urban development for the poor and lower middle-class people in ways that could stimulate their ambition toward being more productive as contrasted to old-fashioned concentrated public housing. The people who administered the grants, though, frequently had no training in housing or urban development. They did, however, know how to distinguish a Republican campaign contributor from applicants who had not met that criterion. As a result, some of the HUD programs were filled with corruption for which the criminal prosecutions and missed opportunities have still not been completed.

In order to provide for well-placed subsidies, it is helpful to have people who are not only trained in the substance of what they are administering such as housing and urban development, but also more generalized training in systematic public policy evaluation. The training does not have to be part of a formal degree program. It could be training offered within the Department of Housing and Urban Development or the Office of Personnel Management. It should, however, be more than a half-day or a weekend. It should probably involved at lease the equivalent of a semester of solid reading, discussion, and lectures by practitioners and academics who have some recognized expertise in the substantive area and the general evaluative procedures.

The supply-side policies of the 1980's were clearly not as successful as they could have been. Maybe they were not successful at all if the goal was to reduce the deficit. Nevertheless, President Reagan deserves considerable credit for having been the first president (and not likely to the be the last) to have super-optimizing philosophy that emphasizes expanding the GNP-pie as a way of enabling the rich and poor to both come out ahead rather than think in terms of trade-offs. That SOS orientation can also apply to blacks and whites, females and males, north and south, and other categories of people who are traditionally thought of as being in conflict over a relatively fixed pie. President Reagan did succeed in arriving at a super-optimum solution in foreign policy by bringing about the arms control agreements. They made both the United States and the Soviet Union better off than their best expectations, although the full benefits of the peace dividends have not yet been received. President Reagan seems to have been a more imaginative thinker on these SOS-related ideas than either the Republican or Democratic candidate who ran for the presidency to replace him.

C. Some Experiences from Great Society Legislation

In addition to strings attached, big money, and competent personnel, there are other causal factors that have already been observed in the short time that the American government has been experimenting with SOS-related policies. The above examples mainly involve Republicans. A good example involving Democrats as the key policymakers is the air pollution legislation of 1972, which is closely associated with Senator Edmund Muskie, a would-be Democratic candidate for president. As with President Reagan, Senator Muskie deserves credit for innovative SOS thinking but one should still recognize possible errors that interfered with effective implementation. More specifically, we are referring to the provisions in the air pollution legislation designed to stimulate the development of the electric automobile.

The electric automobile if it were effective would be a super-optimum solution to many problems simultaneously, including pollution, energy, and the sagging automobile industry. An electric automobile does not have an internal combustion engine. It runs on a big battery, or a small battery with big storage power. It therefore does not spew cancer-causing exhaust fumes. It does not run on gasoline, and thus it is not dependent on Arab countries or the oil companies. The price of an effective electric automobile would probably be substantially less than an internal combustion automobile. That would be good for consumers and the volume of automobile sales, possibly with an even better profit ratio.

The big problem with present electric cars is that they either require a long extension cord like the electric cars in the Dodgem rides in amusement parks or they require inconvenient recharging every few miles. The object is to develop a battery that will store enough electricity so that a car can go about 450 miles without recharging. That is the distance that internal combustion cars can generally go without needing more gasoline, figuring 30 miles to the gallon and a 15 gallon tank. Batteries can now be created that will move a motor vehicle 450 miles without recharging, but one needs to attach a truck to the back of one's car to carry the huge battery, which is not a very efficient way to travel. It just so happens that although the electricity field has seen amazing developments over the last 150 years such as electric lights, radio-TV phonographs, movie projectors, refrigerators, telephones, computers, etc., there has been virtually no great breakthroughs in the storage battery since Mr. Volta invented the voltaic cell in the early 1800's. We now have dry batteries instead of his wet battery, but they do not store a lot more energy.

If we could get a real breakthrough in being able to store energy, we could not only solve the problem of air pollution due to automobiles, we could maybe solve all our energy problems. That is so because the biggest obstacle to using large-scale solar energy is our inability to store solar energy for rainy days. It has been proposed to build a large microwave in the sky above the cloud layer, and then never have to worry about rainy or cloudy days. The microwave would tilt slightly every second toward a different place on earth and send a laser beam of solar energy through the clouds to Dusseldorf, Tokyo, Chicago, etc. Unfortunately with current technology, the microwave platform would have to be about a mile square. We are having a great deal of trouble getting platforms in the sky that are ten feet square, let alone 5,280 feet square. The cost is horrendous. We would not need any microwave in the sky if we had big storage batteries on earth. All we would need is a lot of saucer contraptions and solar-cell devices to pick up the sun when it is shining and store its energy for the cloudy days.

In 1972, the air pollution legislation sought to stimulate the development of a powerful battery that would be small enough to fit into cars and inexpensive enough to be affordable by the average person. The traditional way to stimulate such a development has been to promise the inventor a monopolistic patent. The idea of monopolistic patents as incentives was one of the innovative contributions of the founding fathers of the United States since they incorporated the idea into Article 1 of the Constitution. For about 100 years, the monopolistic patent did serve the purpose of stimulating technological innovation. As of the 20th century, though, there have probably been more cases where innovative inventors have been discouraged by the patent system. What now often happens is an imaginative thinker develops a truly new and useful idea. He or she then seeks to patent or market it, and is sued by a big corporation that has a related patent. The imaginative inventor can not hold out for ten years and a million dollars worth of litigation to establish his or her idea as being original and different.

Senator Muskie (as a precursor of the well-placed subsidy) specified in his 1972 air pollution legislation that the stimulant to inventing this highly useful storage battery would be a statutorily specified guarantee that the inventor would be able to count on the federal government replacing its fleet of motor vehicles with the new battery-driven electric cars and trucks. That is a subsidy that may amount to billions of dollars with just the federal government as a customer, but much more than that since with the federal prize, one could then service the world market for trillions of dollars.

This is a well-placed subsidy in the sense that (for one thing) it has strings attached. It specifies that the battery must enable a car to go about 450 miles, be small, and be inexpensive. It has big money as a reward. It is also being administered by the National Academy of Sciences. They are competent people when it comes to examining battery inventions, or at least they know where to find the right physicists and engineers. It even has super-optimum characteristics. Conservatives generally want to retain the patent system. Liberals want it abolished or greatly modified. The conservative approach may stimulate some inventiveness, even though the inventor may have a false notion of what is involved in getting and marketing a patentable product. The liberal approach may stimulate desirable competition among firms in an industry that might otherwise be controlled by a patent-holder. The well-placed subsidy can stimulate inventiveness while at the same time not providing a stultifying monopoly.

In spite of those good characteristics of this kind of subsidy, no one has come forward to collect the prize. What is wrong? One could say that maybe it is technologically too difficult. One could also say that maybe this is not such a well-placed subsidy after. The defect here is that the subsidy is only obtained after one has succeeded in developing the technological innovation. No provision was made for setting up a system of grants to enable physicists, engineers, and other would-be inventors of various relevant aspects to obtain funding to develop components and stages that would eventually lead to the final desired product. What is needed is a program somewhat like the National Science Foundation or the National Institutes of Health. They both provide grants for pure research and some applied research. Their grants are not big enough to develop an atomic bomb or to put a man on the moon, but big enough to move research incrementally in the right direction.

What may be lacking in delegating this kind of funding to the National Science Foundation is a need for encouraging unconventional thinking. A big problem with the NSF that makes its subsidies often not so well-placed is that virtually all its subsidies must pass the test of peer review or review by other experts in one's field. That is clearly an improvement on review by patronage personnel emphasizing partisan loyalty. The people who participate as reviewers in peer review, however, may be overly sensitive to applicants who propose to do something that will make the conventional experts look wrong or unimaginative. In other words, what may be needed is review of grant applications by technical experts in the Department of Energy who are not academics with sensitive egos, and who will be able to welcome unconventional but possibly promising grant applications.

D. Successful SOS Experiences

The above examples from the 30% tax cut, Enterprise Zones, HUD grants, and subsidies for electric cars were all defective in some important way. Perhaps no well-placed subsidy or tax break can be perfect. We need to learn form past experiences as to how future subsidies and tax breaks can be made better. We also need to avoid the paralysis that might come from over-emphasizing past mistakes. It may be better to try to achieve an imaginative well-placed subsidy or tax break and only get halfway to one's goal than to resort to (1) conservative do-nothing approaches, (2) liberal over-regulation approaches, or (3) half-hearted compromises.

We should also note that there have been a number of liberal and conservative policies adopted within the last 20 years that could qualify as successful super-optimum solutions. One example is the rent supplement policy for dealing with low-income housing. The traditional conservative approach is to leave low-income housing to the marketplace where such housing is understandably non-existent since private enterprise cannot afford to provide decent housing to poor people without government help. The traditional liberal approach is government-owned public housing which has concentrated poor people into jungle-like dormitories to the detriment of the tenants, HUD as a landlord, and the taxpayers. The super-optimum solution has been to provide a rent supplement to low-income people so they can rent decent housing in the private market. Under such a system, the tenants have decent housing and an increased sense of self-worth which may result in more productive ambition. The landlords have tenants who can afford to pay a reasonable rent. The taxpayer is better off because the government does not have to build or maintain the housing. The tenants may also be saving taxpayers money by being more productive wage earners, and thereby contributing multiplier and compounding effects to the gross national product. The system also results in integrated neighborhoods and better role models and peer groups for the children. That is partly a liberal SOS policy from the Great Society and the Carter administration but carried on by the Reagan administration in recognition of its value and its emphasis on the private sector.

An example of a successful SOS-type policy from the Reagan administration (besides the arms control example already mentioned) is the marketable pollution right. It was implemented by the EPA under Reagan, although mentioned before then. It mainly applies to water or air pollution. It could involve each business firm on a given river segment receiving so many units of pollution rights. The quantity of rights given depends on formulas which take into consideration the size of the firm, the nature of its products, and how well it is doing in keeping down pollution. A firm that is doing a relatively bad job in generating 500 pollution units may only receive 300 pollution rights. It then has to either reduce its pollution or buy further rights from other business firms that have a surplus. Those other business firms may demand high payment for rights in their surplus, especially if they are competing business firms. That system may cause the polluter to reduce its pollution more than would occur under traditional government regulation, and more than would occur if society relies on the generally irrelevant marketplace to reduce pollution. The system is super-optimum by pleasing conservatives with its reliance on the private market in the buying and selling of pollution rights, and by pleasing liberals with its ability to be adopted (unlike pollution taxes) and to be reasonably effective in pollution reduction (unlike regulation which is subject to easier evasions and delays).

From these examples, one might be able to conclude that successfully implemented super-optimum solutions tend to have the following characteristics:

1. Strings attached if subsidies or tax breaks are involved, with monitoring that is capable of determining whether the strings or specifications are being properly met.
2. Sufficient money to get the job done, regardless of whether we are talking about a subsidy, a tax break, or some other kind of government appropriation.
3. Competent and objective personnel to administer the policy.
4. Proper timing and sequencing of the stages involved in achieving the goals.
5. Support from both conservatives and liberals.
6. Failure of previous do-nothing and over-regulation policies.
7. Imaginative thinking in developing the SOS solution in the first place and in working to get it adopted and implemented.
8. Reading about other policy situations where SOS-type solutions were attempted or should have been attempted in order to learn form past mistakes as to the causes of successful SOS policy implementation.

INDEX

F

G

H

I

J

K

L

M

N

O

P